Modern Poetry in Tra
Series Three, Numbe

Transplants

Edited by David and Helen Constantine

MODERN POETRY IN TRANSLATION

Modern Poetry in Translation
Series Three, No. 13
© Modern Poetry in Translation 2010 and contributors
ISBN 978-0-9559064-4-2

Printed and bound in Great Britain by Short Run Press, Exeter

Submissions should be sent in hard copy, with return postage, to David
and Helen Constantine, *Modern Poetry in Translation*, The Queen's College,
Oxford, OX1 4AW. Unless agreed in advance, submissions by email will
not be accepted. Only very exceptionally will we consider work that has
already been published elsewhere. Translators are themselves responsible
for obtaining any necessary permissions. Since we do sometimes authorize
further publication on one or two very reputable websites of work that has
appeared in *MPT*, the permissions should cover that possibility.

Subscription Rates: (including postage)

	UK	Overseas
Single Issue	£9.95	£12.50 / US$ 21
One year subscription (2 issues, surface mail)	£19.90	£25.00 / US$ 42
Two year subscription (4 issues, surface mail)	£36.00	£46.00 / US$ 77

To subscribe please use the subscription form at the back of the magazine.
Discounts available.

To pay by credit card please visit www.mptmagazine.com

Modern Poetry in Translation is represented in the UK by
Central Books, 99 Wallis Road, London, E9 5LN

For orders: tel +44 (0) 845 458 9911 Fax +44 (0) 845 458 9912
or visit www.mptmagazine.com

Modern Poetry in Translation Limited. A Company Limited by Guarantee.
Registered in England and Wales, Number 5881603.
UK Registered Charity Number 1118223.

Contents

Editorial

We had more submissions for this issue than for any before. It must be that transplanting is a good image of much that is essential in the whole idea and practice of translation.

In the early days of botany and horticulture plants were very often removed from abroad to a home country and set in private and public gardens for their usefulness and beauty. First from the Mediterranean, Greece and Turkey, later from the Americas, the Far East, the South Seas, the Antipodes, plants were brought back and so naturalized in English gardens that, like thousands of words in our native speech, only experts know they were foreign once. So many flowers and words have roots elsewhere.

In Renaissance poetics translation was thought necessary to a poet's education and development. Poets, like journeymen, should sojourn abroad and return with their native language enriched through the foreign. Hughes and Weissbort continued that tradition when they founded *MPT*: poetry in English would benefit by going abroad and fetching home the foreign. And there would be benefits for the foreign poetry too, in being brought, by translation, into the wider circulation of English. Altogether a benign and advantageous transplanting.

The stuff of poetry — love and grief — travels well. In native or translated language, it crosses frontiers of time and space. Sappho writes, 'The moon has set. So have the Pleiades./ Midnight. The hours pass. I sleep alone', and we know what she means. She says what it feels like. And as Alex Cigale remarks, 'The Russians love their children too' – and not just Russians, all humans of whatever nationality do, which poetry knows and witnesses, but which much foreign policy and all fanaticisms do not know or they forget or never take it to heart. Translators in this issue have 'sought fit words' in their own language to get across, transplant into our hearts, what foreigners have enjoyed and suffered recently or long ago.

The forms of poetry, how well do they travel, how are they to be transplanted? How easily, how most effectively, can you pass from a French line of verse, scanned by number of syllables, or a Latin, scanned by the quantity of the vowels, into an English line scanned by accent? Can you transplant the Asclepiad, the Sapphic, the Alcaic ode? Should rhymes be migrated ? Always? Exactly? What about the traditional *levels* of poetry, the high, the middle, the low, the subjects, diction, gestures appropriate to each? How closely can you judge the tone of voice of your foreign and perhaps very ancient poet? Will you do her justice or make him a laughing stock if you strike a similar tone in the here and now? How much apostrophe, exclamation, rhetoric will your native language take? Will irony flourish in your tongue as you think it did in the foreign? Can you transplant a joke? None of these are idle questions; rather they are the justification for the old view that poets learn the handling of their own language, what can be done in it, through dealings with the foreign. Translation is a school of poetry – not the only one, but a rigorous and rewarding one. This issue of *MPT* is a lively anthology of such questions. There is epic poetry here – from five languages; tanka, elegy, ballad, sonnet, ghazal; there are prose poems, rhyming and unrhyming poems; all manner of crossings-over. Imagine a symposium of all the poets and translators gathered here, the living and the dead, from China, Alaska, Albania, Vietnam, Brazil, India, Ancient Greece and Rome, Israel, Estonia, to-ing and fro-ing from the eighth century BC to 2010. What conversations you could have, and not just in pairs with your 'own' poet or translator. For there are more questions and possible answers here than anyone could encompass in his or her sole self. You would be free to circulate, you would be foolish not to.

An anthology in its root sense is a collection of flowers. An early *MPT* flyer, designed by Lucy Wilkinson, showed a flower over an open book, the seeds of it being released and setting forth. That is an image of willing diaspora, of seeding elsewhere, over the borders, an endless transmission and welcoming in. 'Transplants' continues in that hopeful vein.

But our imagined symposium, if its participants moved in their talk, as they surely would, from the forms to the stuff of poetry, would have to confront transplanting in a harsher sense: as violent deracination, as expulsion, forced marches and transportation, the spirit of it murderous, no wish at all in it that the life being thus uprooted and dispatched should take and thrive elsewhere, rather that it should die. Banishment, exile, enforced homelessness, the loss of a native language, indeed the deliberate starving to death and extirpation of a tongue, all this has been very often the stuff of the poetry we have published in *MPT*, and is so here again. The diaspora we 'anthologized' in *MPT* 3/2 was chiefly the unhappy deed and condition of banishment and homelessness, from Ovid's day to ours. Still the word means 'a scattering of seed', and seeds are notably resourceful in their will to live. Poems survived the camps by being committed to memory and whispered abroad.

Much of the very little we have of Sappho has been dug up by archaeologists in Egypt on scraps of papyri the dry sands had preserved. Miklós Radnóti, force-marched from a prison camp in the autumn of 1944, was shot and buried in a mass grave. He had his last poems on him in a notebook. Those poems were exhumed with his body eighteen months later and in Hungarian and many foreign languages have circulated since.

David and Helen Constantine
March 2010

The Next Issue of MPT

The next issue of *Modern Poetry in Translation* (Third Series, Number 14, autumn 2010) will be called 'Polyphony'.

Like 'Transplants', the title suggests some essential factors in the idea and practice of translation. Our chief concern this time is voices: the local, the foreign, the native, the acquired – and the strange hybrids that come into being when the language of home is crossed with that of abroad. As always, in considering translations we shall be considering the languages and practices of poetry itself. All poetic language is essentially foreign – 'otherwhereish', as Robert Graves said. We want contributions that will attend to the differences of voices – perhaps within individual poems, perhaps in the interplay of poet and translator and among various translations. And we are not looking for unison. Many voices may make a Babel. Discord must be there, whenever it is true and necessary. Ideally, the issue would be an anthology in celebration of variety, without ever suppressing tones, dialects and utterances it might disturb us to hear.

Submissions should be sent by 1 August 2010, please, in hard copy, with return postage, to The Editors, Modern Poetry in Translation, The Queen's College, Oxford, OX1 4AW. Unless agreed in advance, submissions by email will not be accepted. Only very exceptionally will we consider work that has already been published elsewhere. Translators are themselves responsible for obtaining any necessary permissions. Since we do sometimes authorize further publication on one or two very reputable websites of work that has appeared in *MPT*, the permissions should cover that possibility.

James Kirkup
A tanka version of Rimbaud's
'Bannières de mai'

Tanka poems are short lyrical poems originally from Japan. They are
written in 31 syllables arranged in groups of 5-7-5-7-7.

May Banners

On clear lime-tree boughs
dies a plaintive hunting cry.
But raspberries take
flight everywhere from wit's airs.
Let the blood laugh in our veins,

watch the vines twining
in skies' angelic blueness
azure waves commune.
I'm out! If a sunbeam strikes,
I'll expire upon the moss.

Be patient, be bored —
so simple . . . away with care!
    Summer's dramatics
bind me to your chariot
of luck — not you, O Nature —

    at least, I'll feel less
of a nothing, less alone!
    I die — but shepherds
(so silly) die all the time
over almost all the earth.

    Let them wear me out,
the Seasons — To you, Nature
    I offer myself
with all my hunger, my thirst:
so please feed me, give me drink!

    I've gone beyond all
illusions — it's like laughing
    at parents, laughing
at the sun! I no longer
want to laugh at anything —

And may bad luck have its way!

Bannières de mai

Aux branches claires des tilleuls
Meurt un maladif hallali.
Mais des chansons spirituelles
Voltigent parmi les groseilles.
Que notre sang rie en nos veines,
Voici s'enchevêtrer les vignes.
Le ciel est joli comme un ange,
L'azur et l'onde communient.
Je sors. Si un rayon me blesse
Je succomberai sur la mousse.

Qu'on patiente et qu'on s'ennuie
C'est trop simple. Fi de mes peines.
Je veux que l'été dramatique
Me lie à son char de fortune.
Que par toi beaucoup, ô Nature,
– Ah! moins seul et moins nul! – je meure.
Au lieu que les Bergers, c'est drôle,
Meurent à peu près par le monde.

Je veux bien que les saisons m'usent.
À toi, Nature, je me rends;
Et ma faim et toute ma soif.
Et, s'il te plaît, nourris, abreuve.
Rien de rien ne m'illusionne;
C'est rire aux parents, qu'au soleil,
Mais moi je ne veux rire à rien;
Et libre soit cette infortune.

mai 1872

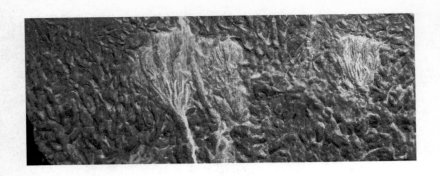

Martin Bennett
In Memoriam James Kirkup 1918–2009
Translations via Italian from the Japanese

In May 2008 from Andorra, high in the Pyrenees, came news of
the death of James Kirkup, poet, translator and obituary-writer
of fellow poets. Just weeks before, in a cut-price bookshop below
Rome's Via del Corso, I had bought a remaindered paperback
of *Poesie Zen*. I read Kirkup's obituary, recounting his early
unsuccess and later brush with notoriety, his departure at the
age of forty for Japan where he was to to remain for thirty years,
his work as both translator of Japanese verse and 'transplanter' of
its forms into poems of his own. One volume is entitled *Tiger in
the Tanka*, another 'transplant' has him converting Paul Valéry
into perfect tanka. Suddenly one of those *Poesie Zen* which had
scarcely registered took on a new lease of life, shedding its Italian
and rising from the page in urgent English. Attributable to the
17th-century Baiho, it seemed an ideal tribute. For all I know
Kirkup may have written another version of his own, anthologist
of Japanese verse that he was. Over the next few days more
haikus from *Poesie Zen* slipped into English, bringing this tribute
into a sort of series. Less translations, perhaps, than 'transplants'.
Or even 'transplants twice-removed', since my own Japanese is
limited to a handful of phrases. Also my own versions lack the
syllabic rigour of Kirkup's haiku and tanka, giving a spin to his

comment that 'a haiku poet is a failed poet in English'. Except that with each haiku came the sense, however wishful, of that commingling of minds which makes translation/transplantation/ adaptation such a mysterious and compelling process: Zen monk, late English poet, this chance translator.

Baiho (1633–1707)

No fame like anonymity,
Life a fretful moment at my back,
Cross-legged within my coffin
I am about to shift skin

Unpo Bun-Etsu

Sixty-five years old,
a monk for fifty-five –
Why enquire, noviates,
where I am headed,
nostrils sniffing dust?

Sengai (1750–1837)

Under cloud-topped cliff, by temple door,
Pond fringed by spring's deep verdure
When a frog, knowing its Basho, goes plop –
Drop goes my pen, wonder this fullstop.

Kito (1740–89)

Seaweed between
the rocks –
Tides a distant memory

Ransetsu (1654–1707)

From the straw raincoat
hung overnight to dry
fireflies taking flight

*   *   *

No payment needed,
a melon gives lessons
in composure

Tantan (1674–1761)

Morning mist –
Mount Fuji
dusting itself down

Tesshu (1879–1939)

Summer meadows
are all that remain
of the boasts of soldiers

Kikaku (1661–1707)

Bridge at evening,
a thousand cool hands
at the railing

*   *   *

Trill of crickets –
Above the trees a travelling
fan-seller takes flight

Buson (1715–83)

A sudden fright –
comb of the dead wife
prickling our feet

*   *   *

Across the snow
lights of the house
that refused me entry

Masahide (1657–1723)

Roof burned down –
For compensation
that moon

Shiki (1867–1902)

Autumn storm: chestnuts
make a vibraphone out
of the bamboo porch

*   *   *

Dew on the potato field
a farmhand's Milky Way

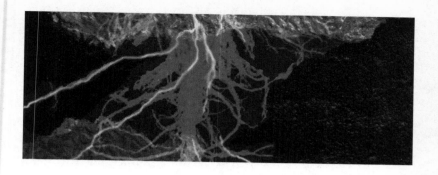

Alexander Barash
Five poems
Translated by Alex Cigale

From 1985 until 1989, Alexander Barash (b. 1960) co-edited (along with Nikolai Baitov) one of the leading Moscow samizdat journals, *Epsilon-Salon*. Since 1989 he has lived in Jerusalem where he is on the staff of the Russian Section of the radio station 'Voice of Israel'. He is the author of four books of poetry, *Optical Focus* (1992), *Panic at Midday* (1996), *Mediterranean Note* (2002), and *Itinerary* (2009), and of a memoir, *A Happy Childhood* (2006). His work has appeared in numerous journals, including *22, Mirror, Znamya,* and *Air.*

Translator's note: What is most human always translates; the Russians love their children too. As Jacques Derrida has it in his *On Grammatology*, men have not the same language but mental experience is the same. This link to our interior dialogue with the self is fairly direct and may even precede language, carried on as it is in affective tones. The pace of consciousness is also consistent for us all and roughly corresponds to the human body walking, observing, working. The events of the last poem, the imagined site of Barash's own burial, take place in the eternal city, Jerusalem, and this suggests a correspondence, an attraction between the poet and his/her 'place of adoption', a relationship that is over-determined and self-selected. I suspect that the situation for the Russian poetic diaspora is very much in line with the experience of all immigration, the poles of assimilation vs. preservation yielding an adaptation. In the late 1990s, Barash proposed the term 'International Russian Literature' which has since proven to be highly influential (for a round table discussion in Russian, see http://magazines.russ.ru/km/anons/club/190509/photo.html.).

To my son

I love you so   that I am almost not
my attention wanes in your direction
I become entirely reflected light
the impression a kiss leaves on the lip

The back-of-your-head smell is forever
imprinted on my nostrils   whichever
side of me you're on is defenceless   love
of you my boy is my only justification in the face of futility.

  *   *   *

In the first minutes of her appearance in the light
she was placed on a table under warming lamps
and I tasked by the nurse with looking over her
Very feminine... A dimple on her left cheek . . .
For the first time in her life she unglues her eyelids –
And we look respectfully into each other's eyes
                                        What
fully-fleshed fountain of existence
bubbles in her throat and bursts forth from under her lids
We finally meet my dearest

*   *   *

When you are ill or unwell
close your eyes – and envision your children
Not so as to gather your reserves of strength
and this accomplished – to overcome misfortune
nor with any purpose or particular aim in mind
But simply so that presently
as from an airless pit
you may reach out and alight –
oh warm nape of my son
oh my daughter's forehead –
and be revived
in the flash flood
of your own love

*   *   *

Terror, perpetual and commonplace   like
the constant arctic night or a sick child
or at dinner time a TV report with corpses
                          (ruined by casual
political commentary)
                          like mushrooms at Chernobyl

It is terrible   oh Lord   not to die
but to live that is to be a human target
The body even when perfectly still
is reflex flux instinct peristalsis

*   *   *

Here they are both, son and daughter, having phoned
on some anniversary date, each setting aside a couple
of hours from their daily concerns, they've travelled
to the cemetery on the edge of a village outside Jerusalem.
The slope of a hill, skull-like roofs, mountains all around . . .
They meet at the parking lot, arriving in unison.
Standing in the sun by the white block of stone each places a
    pebble.
They drive for a coffee, sit and talk about their children,
    about work.
For some reason I see her better, tall, self-confident,
wearing a black business suit, with a bobbed haircut.
May God grant it be so.

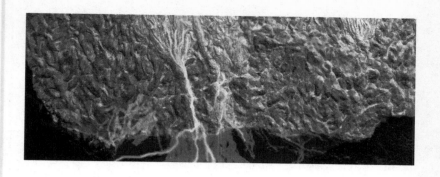

Yaroslav Mogutin
Four poems
Translated by Alex Cigale

Yaroslav Mogutin (b. 1974) is a New York-based author and multi-media artist. Accused in 1995 of 'malicious hooliganism with exceptional cynicism and extreme insolence', 'inflaming social, national, and religious division', 'propaganda of brutal violence, psychic pathology, and sexual perversions', he became the target of three highly publicized criminal cases carrying a potential prison sentence of up to seven years and was granted political asylum in the US with the support of Amnesty International and PEN American Center. He is a past winner of the Andrei Belyi Prize for Literature (2000).

Translator's note: There is no disagreement here; music is a universal language. I approached these particular works by Mogutin as popular lyrics. Just as music contains possibilities for phrasing so words contain their own rhythm and the first three of these were constructed as English songs, in the key of punk/pop. The poet and his/her chosen city and culture would again seem to bear a mutual attraction, in Mogutin's case New York. Recent trends in American poetry toward trans-genre work (emergence of slam, plain speech, performance, and other poetic sub-cultures) represent the influences of American popular

culture and encourage expansion of language into related genre
and forms, what might be called multi-media and collaborative
work, colonizing the disciplines of visual art and music (and
this in consonance with early experimental Russian work, the
examples of Krucheonykh, Khlebnikov, and Mayakovsky in the
realms of art, design, and theatre).

I live in a strange house . . .

I live in a strange house
I sleep on a strange mattress
Strange that no one pursues me
Strange that no one grabs me

Strange, here they are tolerant
Strange that here they praise me
Strange how hard and often
at night they bone me

Strange that I am fed
Strange how I am paid
Strange that I am laid
in this strange bed

I sleep in such a strange house
I sleep on such a strange mattress
often in pain and sadness
I won't for long be around

What I mean to tell you is
there's not enough of me to go around

people

spread apart their legs
find a warm place
to put their hands
getting tighter tighter
it's hurting hurting

people
put to the wheel their shoulders
tense their knees and their elbows
stretch their bits and their bridles
you are the dough not yet risen
and I am the yeast

jesus jesus
we can't get a thing going
we can't get a thing started
the night's already coming on
but nothing's going on between us

people
arch their backs up
and make their hips round
somebody's face to a pulp beaten
their neck wrung
their rib cage broken

here's the window pane . . .

here's the pane pane
window window
I wanted to get in bed
what's there to do?
slumber

he she it
decide nothing
what did I say?
love scares me
no — what did he say?
decide nothing
don't even look but
what's there to do?
slumber

I was talking talking talking
he was leaving running off driving
I warned him right off
that I hate to wait

I never to no one nothing
you ran over embraced — loved me
saying not a word
how lovely then and again over
though I insisted on one and the same:
slumber

you broke down collapsed
I remained standing
impossible to sleep with you so I didn't
even though I so wanted to
slumber

If I was an American

'Russian slaves are highly recommended . . .'
(From a conversation between two Americans)

If I was a American
I'd also have a Russian slave

I would tell him: Hey, Mogutin!
Why are your insides so wooden?!
I'd yell at him: Hey, Russian!
Why is your anus Lilliputian?
I'd not let him off his harness
I'd load on him a gargantuan
                    physical burden

I'd put him in a pair of shackles
whip first with a knout and then with lashes
I'd strangle him with my sweaty knuckles
I'd slowly slice his jugular
Then cap him with a round
                    from an automatic

If I was an American!

Gábor T. Szántó
'whose tongue?'
Translated by Dániel Dányi

Gábor T. Szántó, novelist, poet, essayist, born Budapest in 1966, belongs to the third generation of postwar Jewish Hungarian writers.

Szántó has a degree in political science and jurisprudence from Eötvös Loránd University and he is the editor-in-chief of the Hungarian-Jewish cultural and political monthly *Szombat* (Shabbat), founded in 1989.

He has published several books, among them a novel, *Keleti pályadvar, végállomas (Eastern Station, Last Stop)*, in 2002, and short stories, *Lágermikulás (The Crunch of Empty Boots)*, in 2004. His stories and essays have been translated into English, Dutch, German, Italian, Romanian, Bulgarian and Russian. His poems have appeared in English and Hebrew literary reviews.

whose tongue?

whose tongue is this
you let loose in my mouth?
whose tongue is this
that I am to speak to you?

in this tongue I can't evince myself I can't
shout
cold walls dampen to my voice
stuffed into my mouth
whose tongue is this?
in this tongue of myself unaware
this tongue my mother-tongue my father-tongue
not mine
tongue of theirs
or of none.
training me
to silence
to oblivion

their tongue their words
through it they possess me
forgetting who I had once been
trying to speak this tongue until
it was retracted
this tongue of theirs
forgetful tongue
or of none
lumping my throat
here I cough up
my mucous words
eventually my mouth fills
but my eyes are dry
shedding only words
drowning
remembering

that tongue of mine
I do reclaim hereby

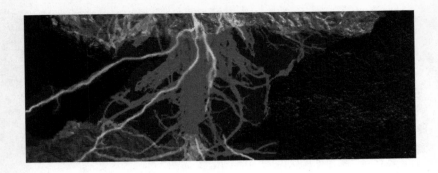

Hubert Moore and Nasrin Parvaz
Four translations from Farsi

After execution

The rape had frozen the heart.
The interrogator had summoned.
She had received this thing.

Also, the cold closing
of heaven's gate as she came,
now no longer a virgin.

All that was left next morning
was a cardboard box
with a girl's belongings in it.

That and the shirbaha, the icy
gift the interrogator brought
for the bride's mother.

Silence

She refuses to answer.
No cry trickles up from her larynx.
Her voice disturbs
not the smallest pocket of air.

Her throat is hoarse with refusing.

At the rub and rub on her nerve
the dry sticks of herself
catch, flame into defiance:

that she, aged 16, did perform
sex acts for the monetary gain
of her family and herself;

that she, aged 16, did refuse
to engage in intimacy
with an elder of the town.

She is guilty on both these counts.

She is not here to answer.

Barefoot

You exist, I love you.
I love you for your dear existence,
not for being mine. What I love
is all and that you are.

I praise you and I praise
your search for yourself: you walking
barefoot through fire to prove
your trust in men's trustworthiness.

Handcuffed, barefoot still, you leaned that day
against the stone wall of the Justice
Prosecutor's office. Kindness
smeared your eyes. You smiled it whole, unwrinkled.

Life, fear, death that day were different,
true to their first definitions.
Hope had a shape like a limb
you could stretch forward to touch
and it touched you back.

And the price for such blind believing?
The price to pay for using
the seven mild letters of the name
for torture – Trust Open-handedness
the Right to Think Unorthodox
Resistance Energy – was torture.

How you paid. Learned the mean art
of living in a hunter's trap,
learned that the grainy ghost that drifts
across the eyes of the unprincipled
shuts them from aims, from vision.

Believe even now, dear son,
the night sky of your love has stars
which shine with waiting.

One should live twice: once
to learn to live and once to live.

In the pit

You burnt:
made a fire of yourself,
made yourself fire.

Down in the pit of making,
its sliced earth walls, its gleam,
there are never witnesses.

Only you of the gasping people
outside the parliament buildings
knew: knew you had found

a flame to cry out the fire
raging inside you.

Note by Hubert Moore

In the transplanting of 'After execution' I have moved the original
'freezing cold' conditions of the rape into metaphor: the rape
freezes the girl's heart, and the interrogator's horrific gift to the
girl's mother I have called 'icy'. The gift, the 'shirbaha', comes

on its own, undescribed, in the original. It can speak for itself. I felt I needed to explain, and, by using 'icy', to win back what the word 'shirbaha' does for itself in the original.

In 'Silence' I have kept the original title, though that leaves much appalling explanation for the poem to do for itself. I have taken up the description of the girl's silence, her dryness of throat, her 'rubbed' nerve, her fire; I have then incorporated what, in her silence, she might bitterly repeat to herself, the charges against her. This is partly to explain, and partly to anglicise: the situation, almost unthinkable here, has been transplanted into English lawcourt language, a long way, I guess, from the rough treatment the girl would have received from the Morality Squad in Iran.

Much of 'Barefoot' seems to me to need no such anglicising. The father's love for his son and the son's lovely ingenuousness transplant easily. The problem comes when the original uses the Farsi term for torture and then finds appropriate Farsi words beginning with each of its letters. As often, I am discovering, transplanting is not a matter of watering down strangeness but of finding an equivalent strangeness.

The poem I have called 'In the pit' seems to me to be about the private aspect of a public act. The original speaks of something like a 'lagoon', in which the burning man is confined. In transplanting I have placed him in a 'pit'; then, again I suppose to win back strangeness, I have given the pit 'sliced earth walls' and a 'gleam. On the other hand, I have kept to literal translating when the new flame is said to 'cry out' the fire in the man.

The original of 'Barefoot' was written by Lotfollah PourAbdollah to his son, Mohammed, a student who was detained in 2008 and finally sentenced in December 2009 to six years in prison for unlawful assembly.

The other three poems remain anonymous.

Literal translations from Farsi into English were provided by Nasrin Parvaz

John E. Smelcer
Saghani Ggaay Ghaas: Raven Speaks
Poems from the Ahtna Athabaskan
language of Alaska

The following poems are from the Ahtna Athabaskan language of interior Alaska, where it gets as cold as seventy degrees below zero in mid-winter. They are from John Smelcer's forthcoming volume, *The Complete Ahtna Poems* (foreword by Noam Chomsky). The son of an Alaska Native father, John learned how to speak Ahtna from every single living elder who spoke the language. For three years, he was the tribally appointed executive director of the Ahtna Heritage Foundation where he worked with elders to produce *The Ahtna Noun Dictionary*. Today, only about two dozen elders still speak Ahtna. John is the only living tribal member who can read and write in the language, one of the most endangered languages in the world. These poems are among only a handful in existence, the only literature of an entire culture extant. To see John's Ahtna dictionary click on www.johnsmelcer.com

While on a book tour in England in 1997, John met Ted Hughes, who was intrigued by John's poems about Raven, especially the bilingual ones. Within months, Hughes personally published a small chapbook of John's poems entitled *Raven Speaks*.

Spring on the Yukon

An old man standing on a riverbank
watching icebergs float downriver,
like polar bears swimming to the sea.

Smiling, he waves goodbye to them.

Farewell winter!
Farewell cold and darkness!

Welcome, welcome
summer.

DAAN' K'E NIKAH TUU'

C'etiyi yihwnighi'aa k'e sdaghaay
ten delzaghi 'aen tayalaeł daa',
k'e tsaani ggay bae natu'.

Dlok', dela' ghełnaa xonahang.

Xonahang xay!
Xonahang dlii 'eł ghaetl'!

Dalasdii, dalasdii
saen.

What I learned from the stars

There are as many stars in a clear night sky
as there are trials in our lives and tests of our love.

Nothing else is eternal.

SII UZADALTS'ET SON'

Nelt'e'ne kilaen son' tah yazaan
k'e dzes tah ne niic 'eł dzes tah ne ts'aat.

'Udii lae kole cu.

Playing hide-and-seek with Raven

While Porcupine counted to ten
Raven hid behind a spruce tree
and turned himself into a cow caribou.

Poor Porcupine never figured it out.

NIŁCA' STANA'STNEŁ'IISI
KAE SAGHANI GGAAY

Nuuni taak k'e hwlazaan
Saghani Ggaay koł'ii niidze ts'abaeli
'eł cic'uunen udzih yats'iidi.

Nuuni tege 'sdade'estniige.

Owl & Mouse

Owl swooped down and caught
an unwary mouse at midnight.

As Owl flew away Mouse pleaded,
'Please don't eat me. I don't want to die.'

Owl replied without sympathy,

'You can't always get what you want.'

BESIINI 'EŁ DLUUNI

Besiini luun' Dluuni tets niidze.

Hwna Besiini t'ak Dluuni kaet,
'Tsin'aen sii 'uyeh k'on. Sii 'uyeh laa laak.'

Besiini yaa c'ahwdi'aadze',

'Ts'e' betanininiic.'

The dandelion blossom

During midsummer, a fluffy seed thought,
'I'm tired of being adrift on the wind.'

Presently, a dandelion blossomed in the sun.

DANDELION C'ET'AAN' 'UNETNIIGI

Ts'isaenniidze, dik'aagi ninic'ezet,
'unitesdzet ts'ii.'

Xukahts'en', ditsiic c'et'aan' unetniigi tah dzaen na'aaye'.

Beaver Story

I want to tell you a strange but true story.

You may think beavers eat only trees and wood, but

> I've seen them eat meat.
> I've seen them eat salmon.

I was fishing for salmon on Clearwater Creek.

> Just then, I heard a loud noise.
> I walked along toward the noise.

A beaver was eating the heads of dead, spawned salmon.

> Only their heads!

I don't know what it means.

TSA' TS'UTSAEDE

Sii idzii hwdzaxgu ts'utsaede.

Nuhc'ezet tsa k'on ts'aebeli 'eł decen

    Sii 'aen tsa' k'on c'etsen'.
    Sii 'aen tsa' k'on łuk'ae.

Sii t'aa łuk'ae gha Una' Tsaas C'ilaen Na'.

    Xonagu, dahwdetnes.
    Ghayaał ts'en lae.

Tsa' k'on dadzaasi tsi.

      K'axonadze' tsi!

U'eł 'sdade' estniige.

Maurice Riordan
Three translations from Irish

Praise for the Young O'Briens
By Lochlainn Óg Ó Dálaigh, c. 1550

Proud I am to praise young men,
Three who've won my favour,
The latest sons in Blod's long line,
Comely lads schooled in valour.

Slim boys who came to my chamber
To bind an old allegiance,
Three young males, softly spoken,
Of distinguished countenance.

I have pledged them each a gift,
In keeping with their high birth
And destiny as warriors:
A poem well-worked in their honour.

The oldest, Tadg, is Donal's heir,
Chieftain of Tal and its clan.
Trained in the art of warfare,
Fresh sap from the root of Brian.

Conor the sons of Cash will head.
He'll be their chief in Thomond.
I give this pledge under God,
Lest some pretender comes.

The third kernel in this cluster
Is Murty's son, Tadg Junior.
Now a friend to poets in youth,
His fame will grow in men's mouths.

These three will make a fosse
To shield the children of Cash.
No one but a poet shall broach
The triple-fence of thriving oaks.

Three hawks darkening the sky,
Unerring in vengeful flight.
Sprung from our native forest,
Swift birds from the one roost.

Three ruggéd bears in the maul,
Defenders of Maicnia's fort.
Three spearheads in the assault,
A match for Munster's foes.

Three plunderers of Fionn's salmon,
Three pips from the gold-skinned apple,
Three buds blossoming into verse,
Three mirrors for a girl's kiss.

Three hazels from the nutgrove,
Three streams fresh from granite caves,
Fruit of the ancient vineyard,
Runnels of juice from the orchard.

Before long their javelins
Will whistle throughout Conn's Half.
In fights where wounds are given
Blood will stain their hands.

Soon they'll swap hurling-sticks
For swords with ivory hilts.
It will make a fair exchange,
Bringing concord to the Maigue.

These young men meet at my side,
Three warriors in youth's attire.
Three horsemen from Brian's stable
Who'll ride with golden bridles.

White sparks from the firing-kiln
They'll shoot through Banba's realm.
Men will follow in their steps,
Fearless to join the contest.

It's no flaw in finished gold
To start out molten at the forge.
To be pliable from the fire
Brands them as O'Briens.

Their torsos white as spindrift,
Six strong and supple calves,
Six feet swift and nimble,
Six fine hands to kindle love.

Six cheeks that never blushed,
Six eyes quietly observant.
Not known to spurn suppliants,
The crowd hangs upon their words.

Conor with the fair complexion,
Two Tadgs, the poets' patrons,
Each with a royal bard at ease,
Three I've singled out for praise.

The Trinity grant them strength,
Stewardship of our holy ground.
May they bring the people wealth.
To have praised them makes me proud.

Note

The original dates from the bardic period, which in Ireland lasted from about 1200 to 1600. Poets such as Ó Dálaigh (O'Daley) were trained professional craftsmen in the service of the local chieftains. They wrote countless praise-poems in elaborately wrought, fiercely conventional, learned verse. This poem is a typical specimen, but it has, I think, an unusually personal and affectionate quality. I was hoping to capture that, as well as catching a glimpse of a splendidly half-barbarous semi-heroic world.

The New Poetry
By Eochaidh Ó Heoghusa, 1603

Praise be! A turn for the better,
A sudden shift in the weather.
If I don't tap into this new racket
I could end up out of pocket.

Good riddance, then, to the old measures,
To those fussy rules and strictures.
This method's cushier, more enlightened,
And might usher me into the limelight.

Those erstwhile ornamented poems
Fell on deaf ears only – lofty odes
Sailing over the heads of the people,
Like caviar thrown at the general.

If verse of mine from now to the last trump
Perplex the brain of one Ulster dunce
I'll give back – it's a hefty wager –
Every last farthing of my retainer.

Free verse and the open road!
It's what pops the money ball.
I'll soon be paying off my loans
Courtesy of Earl Tyrconnell.

No one's going to best yours truly
When it comes to pap and vacuity.
I'll be out there on the fairground
In all weathers pulling in the crowds.

I've scuppered – what a relief! –
That top-heavy worm-eaten ball-breaking craft.
Though if the Earl gets wind of my drift
He's bound to piss himself laughing.

Let me not ruin a hard-won reputation
For mastery of bardic scholarship and skill.
I'll make sure the Earl (or former Chieftain)
Isn't in town when I give a recital.

The thing is I'm quite a draw,
Flavour of the month in certain quarters.
I'd be gone down that path like a rat from hell,
But I'm wary of the Earl –

Not to mention it was the same Aodh's son
Who once dubbed my strict verse 'easy'.
Thank God he's sojourning with the Saxon.
For the time being, I have a breather.

Those poems I pummelled into shape before
Damn near broke my heart.
The new softer more accessible approach
Will prove a tonic for my health.

And what if the Earl (the ex-Chieftain)
Quibbles now and then with a quatrain –
Aren't there plenty goons about
Who'll shout the pedant down?

Note

Ó Heoghusa (O'Hussey) was writing just as the Gaelic kingdoms,
and with them the bardic order, disintegrated. In fact, he has a go
here at the last O'Donnell chieftain, who was visiting the court

of King James to receive an earldom in return for his allegiance.
The defeat meant the bards – a professional and privileged 'caste'
– lost their patrons and had to compete with popular poets using
a more accessible style. O'Hussey is surprisingly cheerful at the
prospect – and I've followed his example.

Renunciation
By Séathrún Céitinn, 1580–c.1644

Dear one, with your wiles,
You'd best remove your hand.
Though you burn with love's fire,
I'm no more an active man.

Look at the grey on my head,
See how my body droops,
Think of my sluggish blood –
What would you have me do?

It's not desire I lack.
Don't bend low like that again.
Love will live without the act
Forever, slender minx.

Withdraw your lips from mine,
Strong as the inclination is,
Don't brush against my skin,
It could lead to wantonness.

The intricacy of curls,
Soft eyes clear as dew,
The pale sight of your curves,
Give pleasure to me now.

Bar what the body craves,
And lying with you requires,
I'll do for our love's sake,
Dear one, with your wiles.

Note

This poem is attributed to Séathrún Céitinn (Geoffrey Keating), a priest educated in France. It is famously 'untranslatable' because of its economy and sly sensuality. It is an example of a witty sophisticated style that flourished briefly in Irish under the influence of the Counter-Reformation.

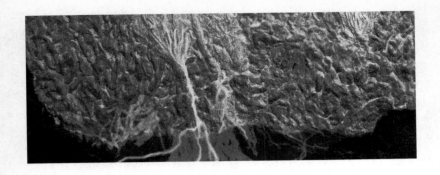

Arthur McHugh
Three translations from French

Rhyme

. . . They may well say that I'm inclined
To flirt with any boy I find,
To take my pleasure here or there –
Well, let them say it: I don't care . . .

(From the French of Pernette du Guillet)

Pernette du Guillet (c.1520–1545) died young, and her poetry was published after her death.

Sonnet

There aren't as many cars in Birmingham,
There aren't as many flowering shrubs at Kew,
There aren't as many trains at Waterloo,
There aren't as many bikes in Amsterdam;

There aren't as many sailors in the fleet,
There aren't as many herring in Loch Fyne,
There aren't as many Geordies on the Tyne,
There aren't as many rogues in Downing Street;

There aren't as many pubs in Donegal,
Nor pretty dresses at a Cambridge ball,
Nor feathers in a well-filled feather bed;

There aren't as many priests and nuns in Rome,
Nor pages in a monumental tome,
As my Marie has notions in her head.

(From the French of Mellin de Saint-Gelais)

Mellin de Saint-Gelais (1491–1558) was a court poet sometimes showing Italian influence. He wrote some of the earliest sonnets in the French language.

Ballade

I'm getting quite a stoop of late,
My hair is sparse, my chest is tight,
I don't hear well, I don't feel strong,
I hardly sleep at all at night;
With runny nose and shaky limbs,
I totter when I try to walk;
My children think I'm doddery,
And no one listens when I talk:
          Death will be coming soon for me.

What hair I have is white as snow,
I can't rely on hands or feet,
My temper's short, my face is long,
I guzzle all that I can eat;
You can't trust anyone these days –
Things aren't what they used to be –
I spend as little as I can,
And disapprove of all I see:
          Death will be coming soon for me.

My yellow teeth are weak and loose,
My breath smells like a garbage-heap,
I cannot stay awake for long,
If I'm not dozing, I'm asleep;
I moan about my aches and pains,
About the heat, about the cold,
About my failing memory,
About the curse of growing old;
          Death will be coming soon for me.

Although my friends and family
Would like me to push off, I know,
I'd much prefer to carry on
Another sixty years or so;
     Death will be coming soon for me.

(From the French of Eustache Deschamps)

*Eustache Deschamps (1346–1407) travelled widely in the service of
King Charles VI of France. He saw active service in the Hundred
Years War, and wrote hundreds of poems.*

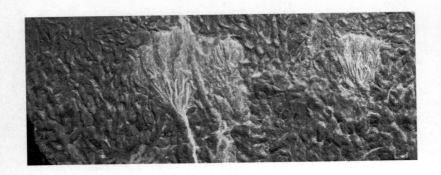

François Villon
Two extracts from *The Testament*
Translated by W.D. Jackson

Some poems seem to be wedded so closely to their forms that
they virtually cease to be poetry without them. Poems of great
musicality, in particular – Dante's *canzoni*, say, or Heine's lyrics –
seem to lose much of their life-blood if put into prose or rhymeless
verse, for example. When translating such poems, it therefore
makes sense to try and get as close to their forms as is compatible
with producing an English poem. The caveat is important
because some forms rarely sound well in the context of English
verse – the classical hexameter and the alexandrine are famous
examples – while others may be, in one way or another, as good
as impossible to re-create effectively. Also, the rhythms of stress-
timed or isochronous languages such as German and English are
quite simply other than those of syllable-timed languages such
as French and Italian (however, longer lines should still sound
longer and shorter lines shorter, in my opinion). Bearing all this
in mind, Villon's favourite ballade stanza, rhyming ababbcbc, is
one of those forms, it seems to me, which one wants to get as
close to as one can – as Ezra Pound seems to have thought as
well, judging from his remark on the difficulty of translating
Villon 'because he rhymes on the exact word, on a word meaning
sausages, for example' *(ABC of Reading).* On the other hand, the

virtuoso version of the form which Villon uses for the *Ballades* (such as 'Dictes moy ou n'en quel pays') which he includes in *The Testament,* whereby the rhyme-sounds are repeated throughout the poem, is only likely to get the translator into trouble if he tries to do the same (witness the excessive inversions, repeated rhyme-words, etc. of Tom Scott's attempt in *The Oxford Book of Verse in English Translation*); and I've varied the rhyme-sounds accordingly.

Ballade

('Dictes moy ou, n'en quel pays')

O tell me in which country now
Is Flora, the lovely Roman?
Or Alexander's Thais who
Was Alcibiades' cousin;
Echo who spoke – poor tongue-tied woman –
Where babbling waters pool or flow,
Whose beauty was more than human? –
But where is last year's snow?

Where is the learned Heloise,
For whom they gelded Abelard?
Made him a monk at Saint Denis –
Love pained him long and hard!
And where's the queen who had her guard
Tie up Buridan and throw
Him into the Seine like a tub of lard? . . .
But where is last year's snow?

Queen Blanche who sang — sweet fleur-de-lys —
Like a Siren come again;
Big-footed Bertha, Beatrice, Alice,
And that Amazon who held Maine;
And Jeanne, the good girl of Lorraine
Burnt by the English... Where are they? Oh,
Sweet Virgin Mary, long may you reign:
But where is last year's snow?

If any should ask this week, this year,
Where are they? Where did they all go?
This same refrain is all you'll hear:
Where is last year's snow?

*   *   *

('Puis de papes, roys, filz de roys')

The same thing goes for kings and popes,
Their fecund queens, and all their sons —
Buried together with their hopes,
Their power and glory gone.
And won't *I* die, a poor bag-man
From Rennes? Oh, yes. If it please God,
As long as I've had my fun,
I'll rest under any sod.

This world won't last for ever,
Whatever the thieving rich may think —
We're all of us under fate's cleaver:
Thus any old crock on the blink
Can drool, who, young and in the pink,
Once joshed his wife, his friends, his folks,
But now would cause a social stink
If he started cracking jokes.

Obliged to beg or steal or borrow
By heartless Mother Necessity,
He gloomily hopes today that tomorrow
His death will set him free —
Oh, but for God's commandment, he
(With his back to one last wall)
Often might have desperately
Put an end to it all!

For if in his youth he made them laugh,
Nothing he says now can or will:
An ancient ape's a horror-and-a-half;
His sour face sucks life's bitter pill.
If he's silent they think he's ill,
Or finally going gaga.
If he speaks he's told to be still:
Who cares for his second-hand saga?

And as for poor decrepit biddies
Without a sou, or fish to fry,
Who see young things with plumped-up diddies
Squeezing them out on the sly,
They importune God to tell them why
And by what right they were born so *soon!*
But our Lord declines to argufy,
Knowing he'd get the wooden spoon . . .

I seem to hear the beauty who
Was once an armouress
Wishing their wish which can't come true –
For youth again – like this:
'Ah, why has age crept up, like a fierce
Thief, so soon, to crease my skin?
What stops me now, in my distress,
From doing myself in?

Old age has left me in the lurch
And stripped my beauty of its power
Over merchants, scholars, men of the church:
There wasn't one who wouldn't shower
All that he owned, his widow's dower –
No matter what – on me
For an hour or less than an hour
Of what tramps won't tickle now for free!

I refused it to plenty of men,
Which wasn't especially smart of me,
For the love of a young ex-con
Who never paid my fee.
He fooled me. But – I swear it – he
Was my sweetest taste of honey.
Who cares if he mainly seemed to be
In love with my hard-earned money?

Who cares if he dragged me round the floor
Or kicked me a bit? He couldn't kill
My love. If he'd broken my back or my jaw,
Then asked for a kiss, I'd still
Have given him one with no ill will . . .
A fat lot *I* got, all the same.
The wicked glutton screwed me, until
Theres nothing left but the sin and shame.

And he's been dead these thirty years.
But I live on – old, grey and glum.
When I think of the good times – remember, in tears,
What I was and what I've become –
When I look at my naked breasts and bum,
And see my body so very changed,
Poor, dry, meagre, gnarled and numb,
I think I must be completely deranged.

What has become of that lucid brow?
That golden hair, those eyebrows raised
Above my wide-set eyes, aglow
With pretty glances which amazed
The shrewdest; and my straight nose, praised
Together with my shapely ears
And dimpled chin; my face which gazed
With hope into the coming years?

My slender shoulders – oh, and those lips! . . . –
Long arms, slim fingers, skilled at their trade,
Small boobs, full buttocks, swinging hips –
A fine high arse, as good as made
For the fine art of getting laid;
Those marble loins, that tiny V
Between my powerful thighs, in the shade
Of its own sweet-scented shrubbery?

My forehead's wrinkled, hair's gone grey,
My brows are scurf and my eyes dull
Which flashed hot looks and smiles in their day
At many a lecherous fool;
My nose is hooked like the beak of a gull;
My pendulous ears sprout moss;
My drab skin hardly hides my skull;
My chins are puckered, lips a dead loss.

This is the way our beauty ends:
My arms are short, hands gnarled and lean;
My shoulders hunch as my spine bends;
My tits are – pah! – just shrunken skin,
My buttocks as slack, all fallen in.
My cunt? A horror! My thighs? The truth is
Their bones are sticks, not thigh-bones – thin
And blotched with spots, like sausages.

– And that's how we mourn the good old days
Among ourselves, poor senile crones
Who squat on our hams by a small blaze
Of twigs and straw, like bundles of bones
And rags. The fire which heats our groans
No sooner flares than it goes out.
And we were all so lovely once.
But that's how it is for tart and tout.'

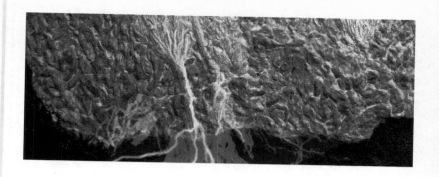

Maureen Duffy
From a translation of *Sir Orfeo*

Sir Orfeo belongs to that long tradition in English of fairy
literature which stretches from Old English elf-shot and the
marsh monsters Grendel and his mother, down through the
centuries via Spenser's *Faerie Queene* and Keats' 'La Belle Dame
Sans Merci' to the science fictions of Star Wars and Doctor Who.
The earliest extant manuscript (Auchinleck MS Edinburgh
National Library of Scotland, Advocates 19) appears to have been
written by some half a dozen scribes in around 1330–40, along
with forty-three other lays, romances, homilies and other pieces
(including a version of *Guy of Warwick*) in a dialect of South
Midlands, London. It retells the Greek myth of Orpheus and
Eurydice but, like Gluck's *Orpheo*, it has a happy ending. In form
it derives in conscious imitation from the poetic tradition of the
lai, popularised by Breton singer-songwriters and translated post-
Conquest into Britain, the most famous proponent of which is
Marie de France, whose *La Freyne* also appears in the Auchinleck
MS and with which *Sir Orfeo* shares its first thirty-eight lines,
making obeisance to Breton lays and placing itself firmly in that
tradition, perhaps in the hope of a wider audience at this time
when English was still in competition with French and Latin as
an acceptable literary language. Its roots are, however, deep in
the English faery/folk tradition which continued, some would say

in debased form, in the later ballads like 'Tam Lin' and 'True Thomas'. The English version of the myth transfers the locus of the story firmly to England. Sir Orfeo isn't the son of Apollo but King of Winchester, and the finest harper in the world, still with the power to enchant men and beasts with his music. Eurydice, his queen Herodis, is stolen by the Fairy King into the parallel world of Fairyland which exists in another dimension into which mortals can stray by a simple but foolish act such as falling asleep, as Herodis does, at a May noontide under an apple tree. Instead of the gloomy world of Eurydice's Hades however, she finds herself in a richly decorated palace where the undead can follow their earthly sports of hawking, hunting and even dancing. We might now indeed call this a virtual world.

In praise of the profession of minstrel, and written to be performed by one, the poem has the effect of a kind of Chinese box or Russian doll, turning in upon itself so that the happy ending seems right, even though Orfeo achieves it by a trick rather than the simple power of song. Returning to his kingdom in disguise he plays another trick, on the steward he has left in charge to test his loyalty. From being a tragic tale of lost love, English has transformed the legend into a parable of virtue and cunning rewarded.

Orpheus, lines 1-322

We often read and find them writ,
as learned men know so well,
tales that tell of faery things
in the lays that harpers sing.
Some are of war and some of sorrow,
some are of joy and laughter too,
and some of treachery and guile,

of old adventures long ago,
and some of fun and ribaldry
but many you'll find tell of the faery.
Yet most of them, as all agree,
tell tales of love as we can see.
In Brittany these lays were made,
found there first, and soon brought forth,
tales of adventures in olden days
of these the Bretons made their lays.
When kings heard from anywhere
of marvellous happenings that were there
they took a harp and let music play
and out of it they made a lay,
and gave it a name as I can say.
Now of these adventures that did befall
I can tell you some, though not all.
But listen Sirs, all that are true
and I shall tell you of Sir Orfeo.
Orfeo most of anything
loved the pleasure of harping.
Every good harper was certain sure
to have from him great honour.
He taught himself to play the harp
and thereto bent his wits so sharp.
He learned until nowhere was there
a better harper anywhere.
No man alive in all the world,
who, once he sat down before the king
and could hear his sweet playing,
but would think that he was
in one of the halls of paradise
such melody in his harping is.
Orfeo himself was a king
in England, a high lording
a brave man, and stalwart too,
generous and courteous also.

His father was descended from King Pluto
and his mother also from Queen Juno
that were once held to be both gods
for the deeds that they did that were told of them.
This king lived in the land of Thrace
in a splendid battlemented palace.
But Winchester it was called
without a doubt as I've been told.
The king had a precious queen,
Lady Herodis was her name,
the fairest lady she was indeed
that was ever seen alive.
So full of love and nobility
that no one could describe her beauty.
It happened in the beginning of May
when hot and lovely is the day
and away have fled old winter's showers
and every field is full of flowers,
and blossom breaks on every bough
and over all bright colours glow,
this same queen, Dame Herodis,
taking with her two highborn maids
went out in the mid morning fair
to play beside an orchard there,
to see the flowers spread and spring,
and to hear the small birds sing.
And there they sat them down all three
under a fine grafted apple tree.
And very soon this lovely queen
fell asleep upon the green.
Her maidens dared not waken her
but let her lie and take her rest.
And so she slept till after noon
and all the morning time was gone.
But as soon as she began to wake
she cried aloud, and a shrill sound began to make.

She twisted her hands and even her feet.
She scratched her face till it bled wet.
Her rich gown she tore in bits,
she was quite driven out of her wits.
The two maidens at her side
no longer with her dared abide,
but ran to the palace straight away
and told both knight and squire
their queen had run quite mad that day,
and begged them to go and her restrain.
Knights and ladies together ran,
Damsels sixty and more
came to the orchard to the queen,
and in their arms their queen they bore
and carried her home to bed at last,
and held her there so firm and fast.
But ever she let out the same cry
and struggled hard to be up and away.
When Orfeo heard all that sad news
never had he heard anything worse.
He came to her with knights then,
to the chamber before the queen,
and saw and said in great distress:
'Oh my dear life what can be wrong
that you who've always been so calm
now cry out in shrill alarm?
Your body once so fair and white
is now all torn with your nails' spite.
Alas your cheeks that were so red
are now so wan as you were dead.
And your little fingers also
are all pale and bloody too.
And your two bright eyes both
glare as a man may in his wrath.
Ah lady I beg you mercy.
Leave off this doleful cry

and tell me what befell you, and how
and what can be done to help you now.'
Then the queen she lay still at last
and began to let the tears run fast.
'Alas my Lord, Sir Orfeo,
since we were first together so,
never were we angry with each other,
but always I loved you faithfully,
as my life. So you did me.
But now we may not be together, we two.
Do your best with it for I must go.'
'Alas,' he cried, 'so desolate as I am.
Where will you go, and to whom?
Wherever you go there I shall go,
and where I go there you will too.'
'No, no Sir, that cannot be.
I'll tell you now how it came to be.
As I lay down this midday
and slept under our orchard's spray,
there came to me two knights
both well armed and all to rights,
and bade me come in great haste
and with the Lord their King hold speech.
But I answered them very bold
that I dare not, nor I would.
They rode back as fast as they could.
Then comes their king to me in haste
with one hundred knights at least,
and a hundred maidens with him too,
all on steeds as white as snow,
their garments were as milk all white.
Never before did I see such a sight,
of lovely beings so fair and bright.
The king bore a crown upon his head
which wasn't of silver nor gold so red,
but was made of some precious stone

that shone as brightly as the sun.
As soon as he came up to me
whether I would or not my hand he seized
and made me with him ride
on a palfrey by his side
and brought me then to his palace,
well set up with every grace.
He showed me castles and tall towers,
rivers, forests, woods with flowers,
and every one of his rich estates.
Then back he brought me home again
to our very own orchard gates.
And right then he said to me:
'See, lady, that tomorrow you be
right here under this apple tree,
and with us you shall go
and live with us for evermore.
And if you resist with hindrance or let
wherever you are you will be fetched,
and all your limbs shall be torn apart
so that nothing then can help your hurt,
and though you may be mangled thus,
you'll still be carried away with us!'
When King Orfeo heard all this,
'Oh woe,' he said, 'Alas, alas.
I would rather lose my life
than so to lose the queen, my wife.'
He asked advice of every man
but help from any was there none.
Next day when morning time had come,
and Orfeo took up his weapons
with well ten hundred knights along
armed to the teeth, all brave and strong,
then with the queen they took their way
to the apple tree and there did stay
making a shield wall on every side,

and vowed that there they would abide
and die there everyone
before the queen should go there from,
and yet from there among them all
the queen was snatched within the wall,
by faery magic stolen away,
where she has gone no man can say.
Then was there crying, weeping and woe.
Into his chamber went Orfeo.
Often he fainted on the stone floor.
Lamenting and in weeping so sore
his life was nearly spent with grief,
nor could he find there any relief.
He called together his barons,
earls and lords of great renown
and when they were assembled there
'Sirs,' he said, 'before you here
I empower my steward faithfully
to rule my kingdom after me.
In my stead he shall stand
now to govern all my land,
for now my queen is lost to me,
I shall nevermore woman see.
Into the wilderness I shall go
there to live for evermore,
in the ancient forests with the wild beasts,
and when you know I am deceased,
call Parliament to sit and choose
a new king for all of my affairs;
so do your best with all my cares.'
Then there was weeping in the hall
and a great cry rose up from them all.
Neither young nor old could speak for grief.
They kneeled down at his feet
and begged him if it were his will
there to remain with them still.

'Leave off,' he said, 'it must be so.'
All his kingdom he forsook
and only a pilgrim's cloak he took.
He had no tunic, and no hood,
no shirt and no other goods,
except his harp at any rate,
and barefoot went he out of the gate.
Oh woe what weeping and what grief was shown,
when he who'd worn the kingly crown,
went so poorly out of the town,
through the woods and over the heath,
into the wilderness took his grief.
Nothing he found could ease his way,
he lived in hardship and poverty.
He who had worn fine furs and pelts
and lain on a bed of soft purple silk,
now on the hard heath there he lies
and covers himself with grass and leaves.
He that had castles and towers tall,
rivers, forests, meadows and all,
now when it starts to snow and freeze
this king must make his bed of moss.
He that had all his noble knights
and ladies kneeling in his sight,
now sees nothing that pleases him
but only serpents slithering.
He that once had great plenty
of meat and drink so daintily,
all day now must dig and grub
before he can find his fill of roots.
In summertime he lives on wild fruits
and poor berries of little note.
In winter he finds nothing to eat
but grasses and roots and bark for his meat.
His body has shrunken and dwindled away,
beaten by hardship, wind and rain.

Lord who can ever tell the pain
this king suffered for ten years more.
The hairs of his beard all rough and black
had grown down to his waist, alack.
His harp, in which was all his joy,
he hid in the hollow of a tree,
but when the weather was bright and clear
then at once he took up his harp so dear
and played for his own delight to hear.
The sound rang out through all the wood
and all the wild beasts came in a crowd
and gathered about him just to hear,
and all the birds in all the air
came and sat on every thorn
to hear him play right through to the end
such a sweet melody there was born.
But when he ceased his harp to play
no beast would longer with him stay.
Sometimes he would see about his seat
and often in the midday heat
the King of Faery with his rout
riding to hunt all round about
with faery cries and horns a-blowing
and with them hounds all loudly barking.
But never a beast did they seem to catch
nor after could he tell the way they took.
At other times he might seem to see
as if a great host passed him by,
a thousand knights all well turned out,
each armed to the teeth without a doubt.
Fierce and bold they were of face
with banners flying in that place,
and everyone had his sword drawn
but he never knew where they had gone.
And sometimes he saw a stranger thing
knights and ladies all came dancing

richly attired in elegant dress,
with graceful and with courtly steps.
Pipes and drums passed him by
and every kind of minstrelsy.
Then one day he saw beside him
sixty ladies on horseback riding,
fair and happy as birds on the bough,
but never a man among them he saw,
and each had a falcon on her wrist.
Riding and hawking by the stream
there they found a plenty of game.
Mallards, herons and cormorants too,
the waterfowl away they flew
but the falcons tracked them down
and every falcon slew his own.
Orfeo laughed to see the sport.
'My faith,' he said 'here's a good game.
There I'll go, in God's name!'
Then up he rose and there he went.
And soon alongside a lady he drew,
looked and saw and at once he knew
by every sign that indeed it was
his own dear queen Lady Herodis.

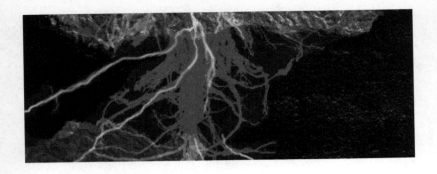

'Ajkuna's Lament'
Translated by Robert Wilton

Ajkuna's Lament

Day has dawned but gives no light,
the sun is up but gives no warmth.
What's Gjeto Basho Muji doing?
Muji is burying his own dear son...

At last Muji took the lonely path home,
where the boy's mother asked him straight:
Our son? Mujo, why shake your head?
You mean you've left him in the green valley, dead?

Wretched widowhood is now her path;
the stars have fixed one life for her: grief.

When at last she'd reached the green valley,
the mother began to curse the moon:
– May your light expire, old sir moon,
that you sent no sign, not a single one,
to the green valley, that I should run
to enter the grave beside my son.

When she came to the grave of her boy,
she saw the beech, three centuries old,
the beech limbs writhing helter-skelter,
one of the finest spreading over the grave.

For boy and branch a beautiful spot;
a tear drops on the dust she loves.
They've stopped singing, the mountain doves,
They've stopped singing to listen.

– And don't you realise who has come,
unwelcoming and fast asleep,
beautiful boy of my own, o?

One last wish, beautiful son:
leave just once your darkened prison,
just one word from the son I bore;
you've never been gone this long before...

Beautiful Omer of mine, o
is it your horse you're waiting for?
Run to play by the church once more;
go and hunt rabbits by Shala's roar;
scale the peaks with the ghosts of the brave;
your poor mother will guard your grave,
beautiful boy of my own, o . . .

Translator's note

'Ajkuna's Lament' is part of the cycle of Albanian highland songs
Eposi i Kreshnikeve (Epic of the Knights); in this part of the larger
network of stories, Omer, the son of Gjeto Basho Muji and his
wife Ajkuna, has been killed defending a castle.

To a northern Albanian or a Kosovar, the *Epic of the Knights* is
a part of identity. Its existence, at the heart of an oral tradition
that stretches back into the centuries, is a legacy of a way of life
and a set of values that still resonate today. In a society that has
lived under oppression for much longer than it has lived free,
and in a language that was only formally codified a generation
ago, the ancient and evolving heritage of the mountains remains
powerful. Generations of Albanian mothers since Ajkuna have
had to lament sons fallen in war, and each generation, including
today's, has found its own meaning in this hymn of loss.

The translation generally replicates the rhyme scheme and
rhythm of the original Albanian and is faithful to the imagery
of the original as much as the creation of a meaningful piece of
English verse will allow. In that sense its Albanian identity has
been transplanted into a new language, where hopefully it will
continue to beat and flourish. This discipline threw extra focus
on the details and beauties of the original; the line that ends the
seventh and ninth stanzas, for example, contains in the Albanian
a remarkable double alliteration, a mournful assonance, and
one word that is utterly untranslatable. 'Ajkuna's Lament' was
translated in the summer of 2009 at Thethi, a village high in
northern Albania, in the stunning and unspoiled valley of Shala
that is cut off for half the year and still echoes with the mountain
spirits and legends that haunt the poem.

Chrétien de Troyes
Le Conte du Graal
Extracts from an English version by Rowan Middleton

Note

Chrétien de Troyes wrote *Le Conte du Graal* in the late 12th century for his patron, Philip Count of Flanders. I worked from the French original as well as using other English translations. The original is written in octosyllabic couplets and I wanted to retain a sense of how this sounds in my version. To achieve this I chose to use four beat lines and linked the couplets with half-rhyme, assonance and, occasionally, full rhyme.

Sow little and your crop will be small,
but if you wish to harvest well
then spread your seed on good ground
where it will grow a hundredfold,
for if you plant in worthless soil
good seed will all dry up, and spoil.
Chrétien once sowed the seeds of a story
for Philip of Flanders, who loved loyalty
as well as Holy Church and justice,

despised all haughty words and baseness.
What is more, this Count of Flanders
was a greater man than Alexander,
more charitable and free of sin.
Moving on, it's now my turn:
I select some seeds from Chrétien's grange
and fill my bag; hoping to gain
a good harvest, I cast his seeds
in your imagination's fields.

*   *   *

It was the time when the bare trees
burst into leaf and the meadows go green.
All the birds of the morning chattering,
singing lightly in their Latin;
everything was aflame with joy,
when the forest widow's youngest boy
woke up and saddled his horse with ease,
took three javelins and prepared to leave
his mother's manor to go and see
the fields where farmhands harrowed oats.
And so he rode, deep in the forest.

The boy left his mother and went to King Arthur's court,
where the Red Knight had just taken the King's cup.

The fool cried out, the girl wept
but the boy didn't hesitate
or ask around for any advice
but galloped after the Red Knight.
Yvonet, who knew all the shortcuts
was a keen bringer of news to court.
He crossed the garden, slipped out

by a postern gate and quickly found
the Red Knight and his horse, eager
for chivalry and adventure.
The golden cup was on a rock,
gleaming beside the waiting knight.
The boy galloped out of the trees
and shouted, 'Lay down your arms!'
'Boy,' said the knight 'has your king sent
anyone who'll give me a fight?'
'Don't you mock me, by the devil
take off your arms and hand them over.'
The knight swelled with anger, grasped
his lance with both his hands and bashed
it down onto the boy's shoulder,
so hard it made him slump over
the neck of his horse. In his pain
the boy let loose a javelin.
The knight did not hear or see
the tip that sped into his eye
so hard it stuck from the back of his head
and his nape dripped with brain and blood.
His heart burst and he toppled down
onto the path. The boy dismounted,
laid aside the shield and lance
but couldn't get the helmet off.
Instead he turned to try the sword
but couldn't free it from its scabbard.
Yvonet saw him struggle and laughed
'What are you trying to do?' he asked.
'The king said this armour was mine
but it's so well on I'll have to slice
the knight into mince to get at it.'
'I'll lend you a hand,' said Yvonet.
'Go on then, but don't be slow.'
Yvonet stripped the knight to his toes,
but couldn't persuade the boy to take

the tunic made of sumptuous silk.
'By the devil, you want me to change
the canvas shirt my mother made
and never leaks for a vest that wouldn't
keep out drizzle, whoever did that
should be hanged.' Teaching a fool's
like pushing a rock up a steep hill.
He wouldn't take the shoes either,
so Yvonet tied the spurs
to the boy's rough-sewn ankle-boots,
helped him wriggle into the hauberk
and sat the helmet on his head.
He showed him how to gird the sword
and mounted him upon the charger.
The boy knew next to nothing of spurs
being used to switches and sticks.
'Take my horse,' he said to Yvonet
'he's very good, but now he's yours
as I won't need him anymore.
Give my greetings to the king,
hand him the cup and tell the girl
that Kay struck on the cheek and cried
that if I can, before I die
I'll deal with him, redress her wrong.'

*The boy met his mentor, Gournemand, and lifted the siege of
the castle where his love lived. He travelled on and became the
guest of the wounded Fisher King.*

The hall was filled with more brightness
than a house that glowed with candles.
As they spoke of this and that
a squire came in holding the shaft
of a white lance and passed between

the bed and the fire. Everyone
in the hall saw the drip of blood
that ran from the tip to the squire's hand.
Sat by the king, the boy gazed
at the sight that passed before his eyes.
He didn't ask any questions,
remembering what Gournemand
had told him about talking too much;
it seemed base to interrupt.
Then he saw two handsome squires
enter holding chandeliers,
made of gold and black enamel;
each one held at least twelve candles.
After the squires came a grail
carried by a pretty girl.
As she entered, a light shone
so bright it made the candles seem
as dim as the stars when the sun rises.
The grail was made of finest gold
and set with jewels, the rarest found
on land or sea, without a doubt.
Behind her walked another girl
who carried a trencher made of silver.
The whole procession walked before
the bed, then entered into a chamber.
The boy sat and watched them pass
but didn't dare find words to ask
who it was the grail served
remembering what had been said
by Gournemand. Now I'm concerned
for the boy, because I've often heard
that on occasions saying too little
can be as bad as saying too much.
I do not know whether this will bring
him good or ill; I do know this:
he did not say a single word.

*   *   *

When the boy woke up next morning,
however hard he looked around him
he could not see another person;
no choice but to get up alone.
He put on his shoes without waiting
for any help, then went looking
for his armour, caught its glint
at the table where it'd been brought.
He buckled up, then called and barged
at the chamber doors, but they were locked.
Seeing as no one answered his calls,
he turned to the great door of the hall,
found it open and went outside.
His horse waited, already saddled,
his lance and shield propped up against
the wall. He mounted up and went
looking all over but couldn't find
even a squire or boy; he turned
back to the gate which was wide open.
Seeing that the bridge was lowered
he thought that maybe the squires had left
to check their traps and snares in the forest.
The boy didn't have the desire
to stay any longer and thought the squires
might know something about the lance
that bled, the grail and where it went.
He rode out across the bridge,
but before he reached the other side
he felt his horse's hooves rise up
beneath him, his horse made a leap
and if it hadn't leapt so fast
things could've taken a turn for the worse,
for when the boy turned around
he saw the drawbridge had been raised.
'Hey!' he cried. 'Who did that?

I want a word with you. How is it
that I can't see you? Come out here,
there's something that I want to ask you.'
But his words echoed off the walls;
it was wasting breath to say any more.

The boy met a girl with a dead knight on her lap.

'What's your name?' the girl asked.
The boy didn't know, but somehow guessed:
'My name is Perceval the Welshman.'
Whether this was right or wrong
he didn't know, but it was right;
the girl stood up, began to shout
in his face: 'Your name is changed.'
'How come?' 'You're Perceval the wretched.
Ha! Luckless Perceval,
if only you had asked the questions
the good king would now be healed
and able once more to rule his land;
a great reward would have come your way.
Let me say this, it happened to you
because your mother died of grief
the very day that you rode off
to King Arthur's court to become a knight.
Many terrible difficulties
are going to befall yourself and others.
I know you well for I'm your cousin,
for many years I was brought up
at your mother's house – I grieve as much
for your misfortune in not finding out
about the grail and where it went
as I do for your mother and my sweetheart
who loved me like an honourable knight.'

'If this is true, how should I know?'
asked Perceval. 'Because I saw
your mother's body laid in the ground.'
'It's a cruel tale that I've just heard,
may God have mercy on her soul.
There's not much point in going on
this way – I only came to see her,
how about we go together?
That one lying over there
won't be much use, of that I'm sure.
Dead with dead, living with living
it seems silly to sit here watching
a dead body – we should chase
the knight that killed him and I promise
that if we find him I'll make him gasp
for mercy, unless I'm forced to first.'
The girl could not contain the grief
within her heart: 'I will not go
with you, nor will I leave my love
until I've laid him in the earth.
If you trust me, take the metalled
road, that's the way the wicked
knight that killed my lover went.'

Carole Satyamurti
Retelling the *Mahabharata*
With an extract from the poem

The *Mahabharata*, one of the two great epic poems of India, was composed, in Sanskrit, about 2000 years ago. Because of its length – the only existing full English translation is nearly 5000 pages long – its transmission has always involved selection and abbreviation. Aspects of it exist as dance, drama, TV serials, comic books, as well as numerous printed versions. Stories from it are told to every Hindu child, and in every Indian language. Its religious, political, moral and philosophical teachings sit at the heart of the Hindu world view. So, although there is a generally accepted Sanskrit Critical Edition, in terms of the cultural existence of the epic it makes sense to talk not of one *Mahabharata*, an ur-text, but of a *Mahabharata* tradition. This fact is heartening to one embarking on a new version.

I am working on a verse retelling of the piece that will be around 700 pages in length, closely based on existing scholarly translations. How can the fascination of a text from such a remote time and place be conveyed to a contemporary reader? In retelling a classic text for a 21st century audience – and one which may be totally unfamiliar with the work – there are several choices and decisions to be made.

First, what is the best form for it? Most existing English versions of the epic are in prose. But, because the original is a poem, albeit one written in relatively plain language, I want to render it as an English poem. The *sloka* form, in which the original is largely written, was a flexible and widely used form. For my version, I have chosen an iambic pentameter template, often amounting to blank verse, seeing that as occupying something of the same place in the English literary tradition as the *sloka* form did in ancient Sanskrit. It is a line particularly well suited to narrative, reflecting as it does the rhythms of English speech.

Like the Homeric epics, the *Mahabharata* would originally have been orally transmitted, by bards. Furthermore, the whole piece consists of stories or teachings told by one character to another. Although my version has to work on the page, I am writing it in a story-telling 'voice', or register, which lends itself to reading aloud, or even to enactment as drama. The language is not elevated, not 'poetic' on the whole, though I make use of the poetic resources of alliteration, assonance and internal rhyme, as well as metre. It is certainly not difficult to understand (though a list of characters will be necessary, to enable the reader to keep track of who is who). In these respects, my translation resembles the original.

Part of what is engaging about this epic is that the characters, and the situations and dilemmas they find themselves in, are recognisable in any age. Of course, retelling involves re-imagining and, inevitably, through a 21st century lens. I have struggled with the question of how far to give myself licence to do that. I feel that it is essential to honour the original text, which must not be used, in the name of 'relevance', as a platform on which to parade specifically 21st century concerns. The *Mahabharata* is relevant enough, without forcing, and the reader has to be trusted to perceive that relevance. There are two main ways in which I have 're-imagined'. First, I have dwelled more on the characters' subjective states than the original does although, I hope, without a facile 'psychologising'. Second, I have sometimes drawn on other sources to conjure up a picture of the physical world that surrounds the actors.

What to include, and what to omit from the vast work that is the *Mahabharata?* The epic has been seen by some as a collection of disparate elements, added over time to an original core. But because I regard it as a unified work of literature (and there are scholarly grounds for seeing it that way), it seems important to reflect every aspect of it in the retelling. Certainly, the heroic narrative is central. However, unlike most previous versions, I have given space to the teachings which amount to nearly one third of the whole in the original – material which offers a vision of politics, kingship and the state that parallels that of Machiavelli in its interest.

The Mahabharata

from: 'The Lacquer House'
(This passage concerns the arson of the house in which the Pándavas, the epic's heroes, are living)

. . . The fire surged crackling
from room to room, through corridors and stairways,
tongues of flame greedy for each other
red, yellow, orange, leaping upwards,
playful, free. An ecstasy of burning . . .

Watching, helpless, hour after anguished hour,
the citizens of Varanávata
witnessed the House of Wealth become a wreck.
Wracking explosions, showering sparks and cinders
lit the entire sky. They flung their garments
over their heads and wept. 'O terrible!
Shiva! Shiva! We've lost the Pándavas,
the jewels of the kingdom, our bright hope!' . . .

When he received the news, Dhritarashtra
was torn, as always. Just as a deep pool
is chilly in its depths, warm on the surface,
so the king's heart was at the same time
hot with instant grief, and deeply cold.
He had not, quite, expected these events.
He and his sons cast off their royal robes
and performed all the proper funeral rites.
He ordered public mourning, kingdom-wide.
No outward show of sorrow was omitted.

See also the extract included in *MPT* 3/12 'Gandhari's Lament'.

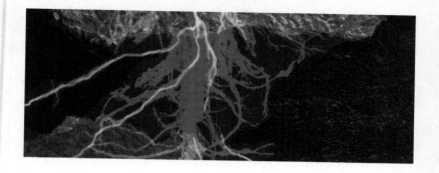

Timothy Allen
From Nguyên Du's *Đoạn Trường Tân Thanh (The Story of Kiêu)*

As part of my work for an international aid agency, I was first sent to Vietnam in November 1999, to report on community-based development projects in the poorest parts of the country. At the time, I had never even heard of *The Story of Kiêu*, nor of its author, Nguyên Du. But wherever I travelled – to a women's support group in the Mekong delta, or to a health clinic in the paddy fields outside Danang, or to an HIV/AIDS project in the slums of Saigon – I found people keen to tell me about this 200-year-old poem. I picked up a bilingual edition on the streets of Hanoi and was instantly hooked. For all its origins in 16th-century China (the Vietnamese original is itself a reworking of a second-rate Chinese historical novel), the story of Kiêu is widely regarded as the ongoing story of Vietnam. The resilience and ingenuity of its eponymous heroine continue to resonate with a nation that has had to survive many centuries of conflict and oppression. In reworking the tale into modern English, my aim has been to bring the power and passion of Nguyên Du's work before a wider audience.

Kiêu arrives in the brothel of Lâm-Tri

She travels impossibly far, across bridges
powdered with hoar-frost, past forests
glowering with broody clouds, through fields
of rumourmonger reeds, whispering and wild,
raked by the knife of a north wind
that ruffles their reed-heads to a skittering sea.

And still the road reels out before her.

She crosses unnamed bridges, climbs unguessed-of hills,
through autumnal forests where red and amber
stain the blue-green leaves. The cries of sad birds
remind her of the family she has left behind.
By night, the witnessing moon looks down
and she remembers her now-broken vows.
It waxes and it wanes till they reach Lâm-Tri.

The beaded carriage creaks to a halt before a gate.
A woman waddles out to greet them.
Her face is skimmed with ricepowder paste.
Kiêu wonders what kind of diet
provokes a person to get so fat.
She greets Kiêu with a bustling 'Hello, how are you?'
and helps her out of the carriage. Kiêu follows
where the woman leads, and steps inside the house.

The room is full of people. Along one wall
sit girls with eyebrows plucked and pencilled;
along the other, four or five smirking men.
In the centre is an altar lined with smoking incense;
above it, the image of that grinning hairy god
who is worshipped in such green pavilions.
The faithful bring him flowers. They burn candles day and
    night.

If an unfortunate girl runs out of customers,
she comes to this god, strips off her clothes,
kneels down, lights incense, utters a prayer,
then gathers up the faded blooms. When she does
all this, many customers follow. Those bees begin to buzz.

Kiêu knows nothing of such places. She kneels
where she is told to kneel, while her hostess prays:

'Let luck and looks and money rain on this house!
Let us dance all day and smooch all night!
Let every man be smitten with our new girl,
let orioles and swifts flock to find us –
let poems and love letters pour through our door!
Let them queue at the front door, let them queue at the
    back!'

These words sound strange to Kiêu's bewildered ears.
She guesses now what kind of place this is.
After her prayers, the old one settles on the couch.
She says, 'Now, come and kneel before me. I'm your Aunty
    Tú.
In a moment, you must kowtow before your uncle Mã.'

'Bad luck has banished me from home,' says Kiêu.
'To pay my father's debts, I agreed to play this role,
but it seems you want this swift to be an oriole.
I'm too young to understand how this business works.
But Mã paid us bridal gifts; there was a wedding;
I thought I was a concubine. I've shared my husband's bed.
Please explain more clearly if I've a different role instead.'

When Mrs Tú hears these words, three demons leap out of
    her.

'A concubine!' she says. 'A concubine then, is it?
I see now what my aul feller's done. I send him out shopping
to bring me a girl — a pretty girl, I told him, a nice bit of
    girl —
and he sends me a creature that thinks she's his wife,
or his half-wife, or whatever they're calling it these days.
I'll teach that gobshite the meaning of the word concubine.
That half-witted chancer, that prick-for-brains,
him and his shagging itch, he had to scratch it,
he couldn't leave it well alone, he had to put his bloody mitts
all over my brand new tablecloth. I might as well
have thrown my money out the window
as trust it to that gormless ape. And as for you,
Miss Flibbertigibbet, I've paid for you,
you're in my house, and you'll do what you're damn well told.
What were you thinking, to let him have his way?
An old lech like him? Why didn't you slap his face?
You're a bold young girl with a one-track mind,
and now you'll feel the lick of my switch.'
She grabs a whip and prepares to crack it.

Kiêu says, 'O endless skies! O vast earth!
I threw my life away when I left home:
now there is nothing left to live for.'

She slips the hidden knife out of her sleeve.
Horribly, she finds the courage to stab herself.
The old frump hides her face in her hands.

But must such beauty come to an end
at the blade of a sharp knife?
There is a commotion. People pour into the room.
Kiêu is unconscious, covered with blood.
Mrs Tú stands and shakes, scared half to death.
Kiêu is carried to a western room.
Someone cradles her head. They call a doctor.

She is not quite dead. Near comatose,
she senses Đam Tiên appearing at her side
to whisper: 'Your time has not yet come.
You cannot escape your duties to the world of sadness.
Your cheeks are still as fresh as peaches.
You want to leave this life but heaven will not let you.
So live. Follow your destiny, frail reed.
I'll meet you later, in the Tiên-đuòng river.'

They give her balms and medicines all day
and Kiêu slowly regains consciousness.

Siriol Troup
'After Goethe'
Versions of Goethe's 'Wandrers Nachtlied'

Wandrers Nachtlied

Über allen Gipfeln
Ist Ruh,
In allen Wipfeln
Spürest du
Kaum einen Hauch;
Die Vögelein schweigen im Walde
Warte nur, balde
Ruhest du auch.

'Wandrers Nachtlied' was written by Goethe in September 1780 in pencil on the wooden wall of a small hunting cabin on the Kickelhahn mountain above Ilmenau. Despite (or perhaps because of) its brevity, it became and has remained one of

Goethe's most famous poems — much loved, much parodied, set to music in 1823 by Schubert, and more recently in 2008 by John Ottman, whose song 'They'll remember you' is played over the final credits of *Valkyrie*, a film about the Stauffenberg plot to kill Hitler, starring Tom Cruise.

In my first version of the poem, 'Wearily Romantic', I've tried to stay fairly close to the original text, though here and there I've sacrificed literal translation for the sake of the sound effects, which are wonderfully haunting in the German. As its title suggests, 'Ec(h)o' stays with Goethe's theme of man as a final link in the natural chain — mineral (hills), vegetable (trees), animal (birds) — but strays into contemporary eco-territory with references to *Waldsterben*, the decimation of German forests caused by environmental pollution. 'QT' is very abbreviated — text-message Goethe! — but, although it obviously moves furthest away from Goethe's mood of melancholy contemplation, I've tried to preserve the sense and rhymes of the original. In 'Mis-reading', I wanted to see how far I could push a translation by ignoring the context and literary baggage of the original language: thus, *Ruh* and *Gipfeln* combine to give *peace summits*, *Vögelein* becomes *birdie* then *shuttlecock* — and a very different poem is thrown up.

After Goethe

Wearily Romantic

How restful it is
In the hills,
So still
At the tops of the trees,
Scarcely a breeze.
Little birds hushed in their
    nests
Wait a while,
Soon you'll find rest.

Ec(h)o

Up here in the hills
it's so still:
trees everywhere
struggling
for air,
birds falling silent in the
        parks.
All you can hear, a whistling
in the dark.

QT

hilltops
decrescendo
treetops
diminuendo
ppp
birds dumb
keep mum
R.I.P.

Mis-reading

The peace summits
are over.
In the hurly-burly
you toe the line,
barely breathing.
Shuttlecocks are squashed in the woods.
It's only a viewpoint. Any minute now
they'll shut you up for good.

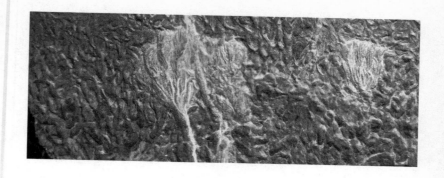

Oliver Reynolds
Poems from Ludwig Uhland

The footbridge shivers as I pass
the alps are flat as glass
O world swallow your pain
till she is in my arms again!

*

The half-breezes are half-awake
all give-and-take
as they murmur and whisper into day
Tonic air practises her scales
lifting the heart that fails
as if to say: Nothing bad, bad can stay

What blossoms, blossoms for ever
never saying never
World puts on beauty day by day
Beauty edges the darkest cloud
thunder thinking aloud
as if to say: Nothing bad, bad can stay

*

Here's the white hart nosing the breeze
as three hunters file through the trees

and then — now — doze beneath a fir.
Dreams tremble on the forest air.

'I eased those leaves apart real slow
and out he bucked. Bingo!'

'Deaf to the dogs' hullabaloo
I aimed and fired in one. Kapow!'

'The pupils dimmed, then died.
I took the spoils. Da-dah!'

And as they wake and chat, our three,
the hart jinking around their tree

eyes bright ears pricked shy head aloof
is gone in the thump of a hoof.

Bingo! Kapow! Da-dah!

*
Life left the dying child
with no hint of bother
like something passed
from one hand to the other

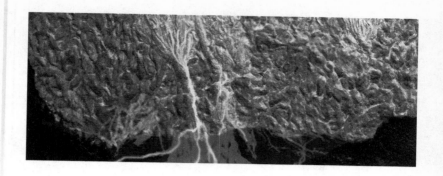

Shazea Quraishi
Two poems from *The Courtesan's Reply*

Note: *The Courtesan's Reply* was inspired by M. Ghosh's translation from the Sanskrit of *The Caturbhani*. See also *MPT* 3/12.

Into both poems I transplanted elements from elsewhere. 'Tell me I am necessary' begins and ends with a line from Mahmoud Darwish's poem 'Two Stranger Birds in Our Feathers'. The tenderness in his lines was the seed that grew into my poem. 'CM' was inspired by a short story by Sandra Cisneros, where the boy at the well came from, and where loneliness is tangible as a grape passed from mouth to mouth.

Tell me I am necessary . . .

Tell me I am necessary for you like sleep . . .
and not like opium to carry forgetting,
or pleasant as a breeze
scented with jasmine.

Tell me what you see
behind my art, my bright cloth.
Look into my face and show it to me.

Tell me what you read in books
and hear in coffee houses,
wedding parties. Teach me.

When our tired, gladdened bodies
drift down onto the bed,
kiss me like a husband
and spread over me an endless blue wing . . .

CM

You are so tired.

Let me take your worries,
your secrets — those sharp
small stones you carry
with you always.

While you sleep, I lift
your white shirt
from the unpainted chair,
smooth it with my hands
the way I smooth
        the tiredness from your body,
                pressing my self against you,
                        sssssshhhhhhhhhhh . . .

I know you have women half my age
– I see them in the street
swaying
like long grass,
their *saris* concealing slim legs
that wrapped around your waist.

Are you my King
or the boy I met at the well
so many summers past?

I watch you sleeping,
my small bed a cradle for you,
my only child,
my only man.

C.F.H. Smith
Four poems from the Greek and Latin

'So like his father' transplants a short dramatic passage from its context in Homer's *Odyssey* to the 21st century. It closely replicates the acutely observed psychological shifts in the relationship of mother and son as he, insecurely, asserts his independence.

'Pelops' and 'Asklapios' attempt to release the mythic core of Pindar's odes from the mesmerising rococo of their language and form. The stories, presented starkly, destroy the comfortable illusion that we can somehow translate ourselves back into the 5th century BC Greek mindset. At the same time the bizarre, unflinching realism of the myths speaks urgently to us today.

'Ad Pyrrham': the classic 'grumpy old man' – and all the modern emotions: snobbery, spite, envy, misogyny, self-pity, arrogance, sarcasm, irony, feigned indifference – encapsulated in three short stanzas of incomparable technical virtuosity. Well, we keep trying!

'So like his father'
(Based on *The Odyssey* Book 1, 328-364

It began with a party. They weren't really Torquil's friends, you know, city slickers, show-offs, too full of themselves by half, not at all my type, on the make, some of them probably after my money.

They had this ghastly DVD on, something imported from the States, all about the War, full of violence. Unnecessary. Well, my husband was there of course, senior officer.

I couldn't bear it. Normally, I stay upstairs in my room with the girls, but the noise was appalling and I couldn't do with being reminded . . .

I put on a sensible outfit – with that sort you never know – I asked them to switch it off, after all there were plenty of other films to choose from. Why do people who make films always have to wallow in blood and horror? It was just too much for me to deal with – being reminded of my husband, my dear husband.

I think *they* might have agreed, but it was Torquil who stood up to me. He said I had no right to blame the film-maker. *He* wasn't responsible for what happened in the War. It was just the way it was. People always wanted to see the latest stuff. I needed to get a grip of myself. He said 'your husband' – yes, *your husband* – 'wasn't the only one to die in the War'. He actually told me to go back upstairs. In my own house. It was better for me to stay up there with the girls and do my embroidery. It was a *man's* business to decide what should be done and *he* was in charge here.

I must say I was hurt, I didn't attempt a reply. So I came
back up with the girls, and cried and cried, for the thought of
my husband.

Until at last I began to feel a little proud of Torquil. He was
growing up. So like his father.

Pelops
(Based on Pindar, 'Olympian 1')

Klotho lifted from the laboratory bath the perfectly
reconstituted body of Pelops Dark Eye, whom his father
Tantalos had served up as stew to please the Blessed Gods,

that part of him Demeter had bitten off (a grossness Pindar
could not accept) grown back gleamingly from a cell of
elephant tusk.

Which so excited Poseidon he carried the boy up to heaven.

But when his chin was darkened by bristles Pelops felt the
urge to found his own dynasty and thus addressed the God:

*If the gift of Aphrodite you had of me meant anything, Poseidon,
help me win the hand of Hippodameia, whose father has destroyed
thirteen suitors.*

*The risk is great but for those whose lot is extinction why should
anyone sit in the dark, stirring the pot of nameless old age, letting
the good things slip through his fingers?*

So Pelops standing alone in the dusk on the sea's edge, to the God of the Fish Spear, who rewarded him with a gold-plated Ferrari, powered by a pair of ethereal winged horses.

And so he won the girl, who bore him six burly princes.

Asklapios

(based on Pindar, 'Pythian 3')

Dazzling Koronis, feather-headed, scorned the marriage breakfast, the hymeneal shriek of the hen party, and her father's orders.

The sunshine-god Apollo with the unscissored hair had taken her. She carried his divine seed but gave her sex to another.

Apollo stood by the sheep altar at Pytho, the searchlight of his brain missing nothing. His sister Artemis the virgin with the toolkit of golden arrows was sent to strafe the woman.

Whatever spirit watched out for her turned evil, those who stood next to her shared the deathblow – a god's anger is not empty air.

But when her kinsfolk heaped logs on her funeral pyre the god said, *I cannot endure that my offspring should share his mother's penalty.*

With one bound he tore the foetus from the corpse, the flames parted and gave him an exit.

So Asklapios the medicine man was born.

Horace, 'Ad Pyrrham'
Odes I, 5

Quis multa gracilis te puer in rosa
perfusus liquidis urget odoribus
    grato, Pyrrha, sub antro?
      cui flavam religas comam,

simplex munditiis? heu quotiens fidem
mutatosque deos flebit et aspera
    nigris aequora ventis
      emirabitur insolens,

qui nunc te fruitur credulus aurea,
qui semper vacuam, semper amabilem
    sperat, nescius aurae
      fallacis! miseri, quibus

intemptata nites. me tabula sacer
votiva paries indicat uvida
    suspendisse potenti
      vestimenta maris deo.

What bony kid drenched in after-shave
squeezes your flesh? Who is it you have
in the cool rock-shelter to mess with
          your brilliant tresses,

Pyrrha, innocent sophisticate? Oh,
he'll curse his changed fate, when the winds grow
storm-black and chop up the sea's surface,
          a gawping novice,

who now credulously takes your fruit
thinking you'll always be his – and sweet,
forgetting the wind's a bag of lies.
          I pity those guys

you dazzle like gold. And me? I've marked
the wall to show I've hung up my soaked
sailor's gear. To the God of Ocean –
          a Dedication.

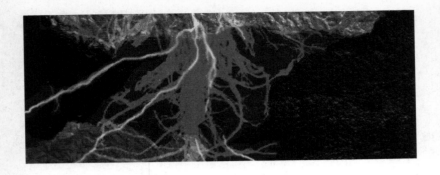

Carol Rumens
Ice and Fire: sonnets for late-Elizabethan lovers

The Birth of Venus

*('I can tell from here . . . what the inhabitants of Venus are like; they
resemble the Moors of Granada; a small black people, burned by the
sun, full of wit and fire, always in love, writing verse, fond of music,
arranging festivals, dances, and tournaments every day.'* Bernard de
Fontenelle, 1686)

Bernard de Fontenelle, you took a shine
To Venus, but we've learned a thing or two
Since then. She's mostly cracked volcanic plain,
Her clouds are sulphur: pray they never rain —
And though the Hubble's filter bathes her blue,
Her oceans warmed and went. Oh, world of dew!

She warns us: cool it. Yet, as your eyes wished her
Life, so we construct her centre-fold
Of continents into the foamy world
Of Terra Aphrodite, Terra Ishtar,
As if such radiance figured potency –
Love-comet Zeus not taking 'no', the shroud
Slick with glycine. Sea or no sea,
Boats burn for Venus still. And gods are formed from cloud.

Alba

It was this morning's REM sleep, and the dream
Began in Kwiksell, or was it Costsaver?
I was near the check-out when, from another room,
He beckoned, held out a gift: *lactuca sativa!*
It was my boss. I was pale and dumb as a foetus,
And filmed with milky saliva
As I stretched my hand to the globe of his home-grown
    lettuce.

Though I stalked him all day in the annex of Human
    Resources,
He had far too much on his plate
To observe the green gleam of my glances.
Oh, let me dream more and lie late,
Till our fingers melt through the lattice
Of leaves, and he beckons me onto his office-lounger,
And offers my lips his salad-bowl, *prêt-à-manger.*

The soldier's girlfriend

Call-up. And it's as if I'd never met him
And wouldn't want to. Others wave goodbye.
I'm hanky-less and dry.
My simple transitives? Dump him or regret him.

I dreamed I found his tent on the front-line.
His face was stitched. His penis would have failed
The *pleased-to-see-me* test. He hasn't emailed . . .
His war has no intelligence of mine.

I google LOVE POEMS, savour crushed desire:
Our courtship, whose whole concept's mediaeval,
Shivers between Petrarch's ice and fire.

Girls with intelligence of love, compare
His tropes with what the literal-minded bomber
Does with the pearls and rubies a young man's summer.

De Chirico paints Ariadne on Naxos

In a household that hid death from childhood,
A boy is handed the dream-death of his sister.
A sheet, dragged through a railing. Harsh sobbing engines.
He climbs in again and again to rescue her.

You can't marry sisters, stupid. You can't unpeel the dead
From their dirty sheets, their wrap of liquefied stone.
But there is another: *puella vagula*, vague pupa.
Ariadne smiles. You un-tangle a little thread.

'And now the sun has come to a high halt
In the middle of the sky.
And the statue in eternal happiness
Immerses her soul in contemplating the shadow.'

You pray in the Casa d'Arte. You have sinned. You know who
   it is
You've left behind on Naxos. Art is brief. Life longer is.

(Note: italicised lines are from a fragment of poetry by Giorgio
de Chirico)

Theatres

Wed to his roadside slut, my husband came
Home in that awful suit-case. Massive-shouldered,
He walked on smaller shoulders
Until he slipped and darkened. I became

A tower of speaking flame, a lilied angel,
Who blushed and looked translucent without help
From Make-up. Tears made little pearls. That helped.
I saw myself divine from every angle,

And all the media trusting me to play
My part – the starry part a young girl's owed,
If she's a woman widowed,

Her leading man all crammed with lead. Some play!
I court the camera's I.E.D., like he
Crawled to that bitch. Theatre's in our blood.

(Note: I.E.D – Improvised Explosive Device)

The White Stag

It was the bitter season — early spring.
At sunrise, on some laurel-shaded grass,
Islanded where the two rivers pass,
A white stag, golden-horned, stood quivering.

Charmed by his glances, I dropped everything
And hurried after him. Bankers amass
Their wealth by being similarly ruthless,
The tough work eased by money's pleasant ring.

Closing in, as his handsome throat turned,
I saw inscribed in diamonds and warm topaz:
'Don't touch! This deer belongs to Caesar's herd.'

It was already noon, the sun had burned
Westward — still I couldn't rest my eyes
Till water drowned them, and he disappeared.

(Note: 'The White Stag' is a re-working of Petrarch's 'Una
Candida Cerva'. *De Chirico's Threads*, from which these sonnets
are taken, will be published by Seren later this year.)

Josephine Balmer
'Arria's Wound'

Arria's Wound

'Both Arria's husband and son were ill, neither thought to recover. When the son died she made funeral arrangements without her husband Paetus knowing, in fact pretending he was still alive. Later, when Paetus's revolt against the emperor Claudius failed, she plunged a sword in her own breast before handing it to her wavering husband with those well-known, almost immortal words . . .'

Pliny, *Letters*, 3.16

When the boy became ill I became a liar.

Paetus was busy – politics, affairs of state –
as he slowly became prey to his own fever.
And somehow, on my own, it was easier,
words I didn't have to form, excuses make;
sweat of night, fly-blown stench of day,
the heart-stop, breath-theft, hammer-blow
of putrid blood in cupping bowl.
I begged Juno, *Mother*, Hermes, *Healer*,
if they could save one, make it my son.
But what the gods sent instead for answer
was the scent of my own flesh on bier.
Even then I still couldn't face the truth:
I'd say the boy was better, asking for food,
take up sweetmeats to his shuttered room,
sit down alone on the stripped-back bed,
eat them, in a dream, one by one myself,
run a finger on his dusty toy centurions
as Paetus, in his own sick room, plotted on,
turned a life-sized army to dust and bone .
And when defeat came, the emperor's decree,
they say I was brave, that I snatched the sword,
plunged it, hilt-deep, in my own chest first –
Paete non dole: See, Paetus, it doesn't hurt.
Of course it didn't. By then I had no heart.

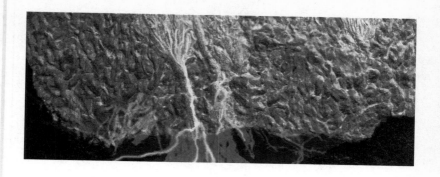

Paul Batchelor
Four poems after Baudelaire

Baudelaire has been translated into English many times, so I might as well admit that my motivations here were primarily selfish: these four poems are personal favourites; and I've tried to translate each of them several times before. This time around, I decided to use iambic hexameter and rhyme – preferring consonantal rhyme, in which the shape of consonants is retained, but the vowel changes: so 'pour' rhymes with 'purr'; and 'stone' with 'turn'. Vowels rhyme in the ear, consonants rhyme in the mouth. I also intended to write each of these as a single sentence (though, in the event, 'La Beauté' seemed to need its short exclamatory sentences) – I wanted to convey something of the headlong confidence of the original.

While I chose to carry over some formal elements, I wouldn't go so far as to call these translations 'faithful': in my version of 'Correspondances' I found myself left with a spare last line, so wrote something to fill in the gap. Purists will object. And puritans will object that my version of 'La Géante' makes no mention of the giantess's knees, making reference instead to other areas. But I've always felt that there was something coy in the original: I mean, has anyone ever told you that you have beautiful knees? If they did, would you want to sleep with them?

Associations

Living temple: forest of association:
babelous arbour: lovely colonnade of limbs:
you've heard my prayers and protestations many times,
now let me lose myself in your sublime confusion
where everything is solved, where all is harmony,
where chimes and bitter perfumes answer note for note
the way a sunstruck dawn answers a moonless night;
a deepening echolalia where, even now,
fine as a baby's buttery breath, sweet odours pour
from colonies of oboes, rise in blues & greens,
and join with others just as rich, just as impure:
an ocean without landfall – amber, musk and incense –
on which we sail in hopeless, livid ecstasy:
homelands are homelands, even those we'll never see.

La Géante

Du temps que la Nature en sa verve puissante
    Concevait chaque jour des enfants monstrueux,
    J'eusse aimé vivre auprès d'une jeune géante,
    Comme aux pieds d'une reine un chat voluptueux.
J'eusse aimé voir son corps fleurir avec son âme
    Et grandir librement dans ses terribles jeux;
    Deviner si son coeur couve une sombre flamme
    Aux humides brouillards qui nagent dans ses yeux;
Parcourir à loisir ses magnifiques formes;
    Ramper sur le versant de ses genoux énormes,
    Et parfois en été, quand les soleils malsains,
Lasse, la font s'étendre à travers la campagne,
    Dormir nonchalamment à l'ombre de ses seins,
    Comme un hameau paisible au pied d'une montagne.

A Giantess

If it were nowadays, if Nature had the nerve
to mother monsters as she once did, what I'd give
to humble myself before a giantess: to pour
myself about her mighty feet; to loll and purr
in solidarity with her heart's smouldering furnace;
to ponder on the brimming nooks of her sad eyes;
to see her — young and daily growing — in the first
flush of her powers; to chart her inner weather, feast
on the abundant valley of her arse and scale
the inguinal upland of her cunt; to climb until,
heady, triumphant in defeat, I'd earned my rest —
then set up camp beneath an overhanging breast
and wait in that thin air for the promised day when
she recognises me her only citizen.

'I will give these lines to you . . .'

I will give these lines to you and some day, should my
    name —
a little ship entrusted to the tide of time —
make landfall on a distant coast; should I win fame
and what I'm writing now survive, then through my rhyme
your memory — like something fabulous handed down,
some tale of a goddess — may like a dulcimer
tease & lull the reader: so you will live again
and, through my sullen craft, rise up & speak once more
to tell of how you suffered their contempt: you
the overlooked: you the looked-over — even as now,
moving with such grace as to barely cast a shadow,
you crush them underfoot: all those who laid you low,
the scum who treated you like an upstart, a shrew —
O my dark-eyed fury, my angel of the burning brow!

Beauty

People, I'm beautiful! I'm a dream made of stone!
My body, upon which my lovers each in turn
received their bruises, was put here to inspire
poets to sing the eternal music of the spheres!
Aren't I inscrutable? Like a sphinx on my throne —
my heart: a fist of ice; my skin: white as a swan.
Being an ideal form means I don't move a muscle.
You will not see me weep. You will not see me smile.
Poor poets: having once known my exquisite body,
they lose themselves, poor lambs, in fruitless years of study —
if only I could blink! My eyes shine — & so I,
with mirrors cunningly arranged to magnify
my beauty, hypnotise anyone fool enough
to take me for a noble monument to love.

William I. Elliott

Translator/Poet Perspectives

He thought his version comparable to,
say, trespassing,
jaywalking, loitering —
some misdemeanour
he'd be forgiven for.

She thought it, contrariwise,
a major crime, hit-and-run,
armed robbery, malice aforethought
with intent to kill;
said, to throw the book at him.

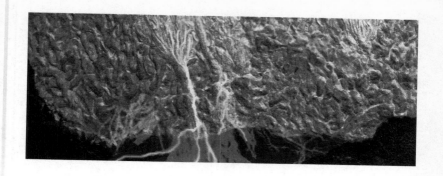

Alison Brackenbury
'Transplanted'

Does a move within one country require translators? I once
read that in (nineteenth-century?) Britain, Southerners needed
interpreters to speak to miners in the North-East. The
nineteenth-century dialect of my birth county, Lincolnshire,
looks just as impenetrable. (Could you guess that 'pronksum'
meant 'donkey'?)

But surely translation is not necessary in the mobile- and
media-ridden Britain of my lifetime? Yes, it is, especially when
money, class, ambition − and a Lincolnshire elocution teacher −
are tossed into the mix. Here is poetry's unofficial translation of
one passage in Britain's official records.

Transplanted

Yet all I took from it was words.
How strange! It was a solid place.
Potatoes, like an old man's face,
clay-caked, fell ruddy from the spade.
Huge sheep, the fruit-crammed pies they made,
now dwindle like the summer's birds.

What did they say? 'It's fairing up.'
My grandfather, his hot blue eyes
pure Viking, watched clouds sweep from skies.
His younger son said 'last back end'
for autumn, leafless, with no friend.
Silent, I stirred my steaming cup.

My mother sighed. They would not fit:
old words, new money. In my head
I hear what Margaret Thatcher said,
puzzling note-takers. MPs bayed,
she lost taught tones, Hansard's 'afraid',
shrieked, to our schoolyard, 'I'm not frit!'

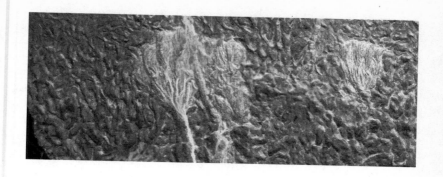

Gregory Warren Wilson

Himalayan Balsam

'growing may require some experience'

I haven't opened the packet.
The marvellous poppies do not reproach me.
They are pure potential.
They have not failed my imagination.

> *What is vermiculite? How long in the fridge*
> *(not freezer) under polythene? What is semi-*
> *shade? Frost may be beneficial but protect*
> *from heavy rain. How much rain? Where?*

I've learnt to say 'the breathtaking blue
of the meconopsis' and believe it's true.

Fifty seeds adrift in a sachet,
fifty vivid souls rattling between incarnations,
less substantial than a wind-thinned prayer flag,
intense blue souls, unlit gas flames.

You have not failed me, nor have I you,
almost shimmering, almost a vision,
implicit blue,
potent symbols of potency,
the purest promise imaginable
and I keep you, keep you, keep you.

András Mezei
Five poems from *Christmas in Auschwitz*
Translated by Thomas Ország-Land

András Mezei (1930-2008) survived the Holocaust as well
as the three-month siege of Budapest. Throughout his long
writing career, he returned repeatedly to the terrible experiences
of his childhood, notably in *Piled-up Time, Dual Ties, The
Miracle Worker, Jewish Poems, Adorno* and *Treble* – assembling a
poetic collage of eye-witness accounts of racist mass murder. A
locksmith by trade, András Mezei was one of the most prominent
writers in Communist Hungary. A poet, novelist and essayist,
he wrote the script of *Lucky Daniel*, one of the first Hungarian
films to critically examine the events of 1956. In the 1990s he
launched the Belvárosi Könyvkiadó publishing house and the
cultural journal *Central European Times*. He was a recipient of the
Hungarian János Arany Prize and the Israeli Kotzetnik Prize. He
died in his native Budapest in 2008. *Christmas in Auschwitz* will
in published by Smokestack Books in June 2010.

Faces

Blessed be those whom I passed on the street,
those who beheld on my chest
the yellow Star of David,
those who were saddened by the sight,
those who walked on with heavy heart
burdened by shame; and blessed be also
those who chose to avert their faces
closed with fixed and frozen looks.

The Lists

They did not need quite 24 hours
in Győr, nor in Veszprém or Szombathely,
in all the small cities throughout the land
a register of Jewish residents
was assembled before the sunrise
the very day the Germans took over –
the lists were prepared in a sense of shame
and helplessness, in heartfelt regret,
you might say with the greatest of sympathy
and embarrassment. They were surrendered.

Poor Folk

If you and your family must be taken away,
at least do right by us, we are poor folk
and to you it is now all the same —
we'll send the children over to collect,
may the Eternal Lord keep you
and we will save your valuables,
in case you return.

The Roma

They could not read the deportation order.
They did not heed the thunder of the drums.
But they knew: immediately, they ran asunder.

Haste

After the Jews had been taken
the gendarmes combed through all of Derecske
and found granny Krammer in hiding,
she was ninety-three years of age,
and also Eve Németi's little brother,
just three years old and a day or two.
They were dispatched in earnest haste
to the rest of the transport still in Nagyvárad
to catch up with the deportation,
so that even those two should not be missing
from the round six million.

Itzik Manger
Four poems
Translated by Murray Citron

Itzik Manger was born in Romania in 1900. He lived in Warsaw in the 1930s. In 1938 he moved to Paris. He escaped to Marseilles before the Germans came, and made his way to North Africa, and then to England. After the war he moved to New York. Then he moved to Israel. He died there in 1968.

Manger's work is entirely in Yiddish. Among readers of Yiddish he was the most popular Yiddish poet in the twentieth century.

Manger developed a genre which he called Chumash Lider – Bible Poems. He retold bible stories in ballad form, setting the events in the Slavic landscape of Eastern Europe.

These poems are from a series based on the Book of Ruth. The Yiddish originals appear in a collection called *Lid Un Balade – Poems and Ballads*, published in New York in 1952. Only eight of the series survive. Manger says in a note that the others were lost in North Africa.

Naomi says 'God of Abraham'

Old Naomi stands in the room.
'God of Abraham,' she says.
Her daughters-in-law are pious and blonde,
And attentive to ease her ways.

'God of Abraham, mighty God,
The Sabbath is passing on,
And like Sabbath in a foreign town,
My happiness is gone.'

Slowly she goes to the windowpane.
Outside she sees the mill.
The vanes are turning hardly at all,
The air is cool and still.

Elimelech purchased the mill,
And the mill ground flour for bread.
Now her husband is in the other world
And both her sons are dead.

Now she is a widow in the town,
Alone with her daughters-in-law –
Orpah is good as raisin-bread,
And Ruth is like baklava.

Naomi thinks back. A pair of shikses
Was what she did not prefer,
But so it was written, it seems, and now
They both are dear to her.

Both of them truly loved her sons,
They worked with them on the farm,
And they loved and honoured their parents-in-law,
And walked with them arm in arm.

Now sadly they are widows both,
And she is a widow alone.
For them there may yet be life to live,
But she, a lonely stone

Will schlep and trudge and schlep on foot
Back westwards to Canaan –
And there the Angel of Death perhaps
Will be her second man.

Naomi whispers, and the widows listen.
'God of Abraham' they hear.
Outside is the air of hay and wind.
Indoors there is the prayer.

Naomi cannot sleep

Naomi struggles to fall asleep.
The window rattles and jars.
Deep in the night outside there glow
Three great golden stars.

The selfsame stars as those at home,
Yet they seem so alien.
Naomi feels her tired old heart
Grieve and grieve again.

Under the alien stars above
She is leaving graves behind,
And her ruined happiness over the graves
Blows in a mournful wind.

Tomorrow at dawn, with the All-highest's help,
She will go forever from here.
Truly? Really? She feels a fright.
The way is not so clear.

The graves plead and call to her:
'Naomi . . . Mother . . . No!
Stay with us! Stay close to us!
You dare not, you will not go.

Not there where your childhood cradle stands,
No, not there is your home,
But here where you covered us with earth,
Each of us in his tomb.'

Naomi shudders. 'O righteous God,
Unriddle for me my ways.
Shall I go, or shall I stay here,
Until my end of days?'

And Naomi hears how the rustling wind
Makes the trees in the orchard nod,
And suddenly and without a voice,
Unfolds the glory of God.

'The dead are only phantasies.
They do not have joy or woe.
And God is light, and always light.
Rise up at dawn and go!

Your God does not wait where the tombstones wait,
But there where your cradle rocks.
Rise up, rise up, at the dawn of day,
And go to where God walks.'

Naomi smiles. The wind outside
Makes the trees in the orchard nod.
She falls asleep, and over her
Trembles the glory of God.

Orpah cannot sleep

Orpah sits in her room at night,
And reads the letter again.
Her father the gray-haired peasant writes.
She reads it over again.

'Orpah, child, it's time to come home,
Your mother is old and ill.
Karase the cow calved last night,
And all is by God's will.

'Stashuk the miller killed his wife
With his axe and she is dead.
Now he sits in jail. Thanks be to God,
We manage our piece of bread.

'Annie the lancer's daughter came
With a belly home from town.
Her mother sobs and the lancer drinks
And pounds the fences down.

'By Itzke the Jew, who keeps the inn,
The windows all got smashed,
And Itzke himself, and his household too,
The bailiffs have them stashed.

'By the way — Antek, the village scribe,
Stopped me on the street.
— Heard that Orpah's husband died,
And she is short what to eat.

Listen, if Orpah wants to come home
— Write to her, let's shake hands —
Even though she lived with a Jew,
I will take her as she stands.'

She puts down the letter. Antek calls.
In a world where nothing is sure,
Could it be? Really? Could it be with him
That happiness waits for her?

Slowly she walks to the windowpane.
Her heart is heavy to bear.
The graveyard sleeps in the white moonlight,
And she weeps a final tear.

Ruth cannot fall asleep

Ruth stands by the looking glass,
And combs her yellow hair.
The words that her mother-in-law said today
Are painfully clear.

In the morning, in a few short hours,
Old Naomi will go alone
Back to her people and her god.
What of her, when Naomi is gone?

Back home to the village, where her father drinks,
And her stepmother shouts and sneers –
Mean-faced Marusia, who has enough
Already darkened her years.

Back home to the village, where the boss
Beats the serfs with an iron rod –
She remembers as if today her brother
Soaked in his sweat and blood.

Back home to the village, where the madman Wasil
Tells everyone in the square
How he was blessed by Jesus himself
On top of the steeple there.

She shudders. The lake whispers outside,
'Come, Ruthy, beloved, come!
Old Ruselka I have divorced –
Now I am frolicsome.

Come, be my Ruselka, Ruth, my love,
Come be my waterwife.
I have waterroses for your hair,
And pearls to last your life.

With me you'll have every luxury –
Nothing could be more fine –
By day, the fine gold of the sun,
And by night, the white moonshine.'

Ruth hears and shivers. Yes, she is ready.
She will not live in the past.
If her mother-in-law won't take her along,
She has a place at last.

(For more Manger see *MPT 3/4*)

Amir Or
'The City'
Translated by Pascale Petit and the author

Amir Or, b.1956 in Tel Aviv, has published nine volumes of poetry. His poems have been translated into more than thirty languages and published in eight books in Europe and the U.S. His latest books in English are *Poem* (Dedalus 2004) and *Day* (Dedalus 2006). He has also published a fictional epic in metred prose, *The Song of Tahira* (2001) and five volumes of his own translations from ancient Greek and English. For his poetry he has been awarded the Peliades honour, a Fulbright Award for Writers, the Prime Minister's Prize and the Bernstein Prize, among others.

'The City'

Translated by Pascale Petit and the author

In the dry dark, the dark that can't keep light out,
     the dark radiating out of minerals, sand grains, eyes forced to look;
in the night-glow that makes the wilderness shine,
     the opening to the beyond, where all that remains are sand-eyes,
that sucks up all that is left of skin, the horizon,
     in the face that still says *Let there be . . .*
there are clay houses, a square, also of sand, and a wall
     up to the sky, sinking into an endless parched ochre.
In wall-stones lost images still bulge to escape
     from the shadow, from an existence whose struggle
against light weakens each day. The fleeting God
     also leaves behind tornado dust that whirled here in the square
and promptly died. The priests, whose flesh hangs on them
     by a thread, are nothing but savage will – a demon that gripped
their rib-bellows and the pendants of sand hanging from their ears.
     There is no more God, only a spell by which
the final promised peace is remembered.
     In the far stars they see others like themselves
with an even older despair, whose apocalyptic prophecies
     are extinguished and sightless.
Now they only look back to selves blank in mirrors, and in trance
     they visit the face of old earth, where the primordial power of words
has waned from too much talk.
     And in deepest night or dark day, they gather here in the square
to speak of the gulf, its glut of empty holiness. Almost bodiless,
     they say that only the flesh still recalls, within its thinning fluids,
lush ferns hanging over water, cicadas, the thrum inside grass
     where leeches and blindworms burst out and writhe among shadows and reeds.
They remember a shoreline, the vast surfaces of dewy leaves
     under a tree-trunk draped with moss and fungi, a rock-cape that in
          dimming light
exposes a Pan under-face: horns of plenty and a snout of is-ness.
     But what's there isn't and their expressions
wrench everything open. Say, do you recall hundreds of years back,
     whether there ever was an end, a death that breathed
life in then out? The sea withdrew into vapour, earth into fire, ether

into what isn't here. And only a crier, a dumb dancer, moving and watching
from the top of a makeshift scaffold, voiceless, unseeable, speaks:
  'I take from the earth only a handful, release, let
the sand fall. See me, reflection, approach, see,
    the dead are so alive, so yearning-to-be; and the world wears their faces like
      skeletons
of hope, and above them some diluted Heights of possible going-beyondness –
    but the *there* shakes and the mirror becomes sand.
The fear of afterwards, the formlessness, the silence
    invades. See, how love between creatures like us
is faceless, fearless, without enchantment; but we don't
    want to, we prefer to think there's still something to lose.
That's how we created a dead sea, the spirit that blows through us,
    the fire that fell here between the I and the you –
and consumes the here like a sacrifice to a god whose face
    we haven't yet seen. Our devoured flesh is spirit.
We don't look at the world any more, and that's how it fades.
    Each name is wiped clean, scorched to a yellow shade
and a post-whirlwind silence like an opening made here for us, greener
    than the memory of water. In the square the priests
mark veins on arms: here the blood is wet.'

The opening shrinks every minute, the gate that gaped sand sucks
    the last liquid, the light-blue, the water-windows
of God's eyes. With a black passing form, parting the desert,
    an angel comes running in the sweaty leaking skin of a corpse
turned water-gourd, and in his hand an epistle sealed by the desert.
    He offers us vellum that once breathed like him, had fur
over a sacrificial beast which we called 'calf':
    'Greetings,' is written there, 'I missed your faces so much,
but I didn't call you; I've nothing to give. I hear you, and my poverty
    falls into the world, and no longer creates, chaos from existence.
What fell, a star or a vase? And what broke, the name or its owner?
    I'm at peace. You? You're peaceful as a sun, and only gazing at your destiny,
waiting in a rimless core. In a short while all will fall, but the "all"
    is only rumour.' Look at the wall: a frieze of naked bodies the wind ground,
leg stumps, pocked curves, eroded human forms;
    the creating eye has dried up, and there's nothing in it except stasis.
What fell like a leaf from the summits, that fluttering
    became silent in front of its resurrected audience,

but paces with this black-and-white age-faded night-day
   turned yellow, yellow. Vein colours, place stains,
behind us the opening from which things seem to tumble like a torrent.
   We're here, breathing, living, in a borrowed here
that has nothing except you, you and your I,
   that you've already forgotten how to give birth to.
To fall, to sleep like a tree — we are
   the voice of silence and fear, a desert of unmarked graves;
this memory, the togetherness and the despair that branches over a wall and a squa
   only waiting to be populated by a caravan of tracks,
like an already broken-in dance
   between the fang and the prey: *He-hei, he-hei* —

Already potatoes and molehills are drawn downwards,
   and our surnames shrink into one vowel *He-hei* —
Save us on High, and don't collapse into your flesh
   like sand imploding inside sand. Everything's finished, but one
crimson line survived on the face of the sand, grew a green corpse,
   sprouted, raised a stem and turned into wood with trembling
foliage, shadows and air-water,
   to enter for a moment a pulse-beat hush,
the pulse of a fruit's opening ripeness,
   the water we milked from the sand, the bucket in the empty cowshed,
the morning in the square in which the priests call
   frenzied, their voices razed by a rage which flowered and seeded
in our flesh like ancient boils: 'Who died? Who died? Who died?'
   Memory gapes open, bends, and in it a waning metropolis
with weakening electricity flickers without being extinguished, and in it slaves
   beat the gong opposite a carved wall whose images subside
into the square emptied of its history.
   At every dawn-line the voice of keeners is heard
announcing day.

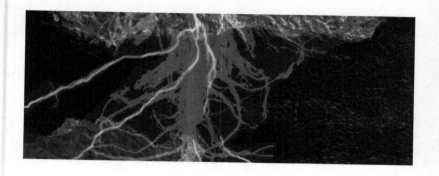

Norbert Hirschhorn

My Cousin the Greenhorn

I had a pretty cousin, just over on the boat, a real greenhorn. Her hair cascaded in curls, her cheeks flushed with freedom, she was the kind who skipped when she walked, trilled when she talked. 'Listen greenhorn,' I warned, 'this may be the *goldene medine*, but it's no land of milk and honey. The streets are pocked, the men are goats, you've no *mama,* no *tate* to watch out for you.' Yet her feet begged to dance, her eyes to flirt, and no bent-backed tailor or pasty-faced scholar for her, God forbid! But you can't eat gaiety. Soon she was tied to a machine, working for some lecher himself once green. Meantime, I had my own troubles, so when I saw her again her feet were wrapped in ragged slippers, her hair cut blunt, her cheeks, once like pomegranates, now sunken and sallow, her belly swollen. '*Nu*, greenhorn, how goes it?' She stared past me as if not knowing that anyone spoke. Finally: 'To hell with your *goldene medine!*'

Note: This is a recomposition of a Yiddish popular song, 'Di Grine Kuzine', music by Abe Schwartz (1881-1963), lyrics by Hyman (Khayim) Prizant. A perennial favourite for Klezmorim.

Original song and literal translation:

Tsu mir iz gekumen a kuzine
Sheyn vi gold iz zi geven, di grine
Bekelakh vi royte pomerantsn
Fiselakh vos betn zich tsum tantsn.

A girl cousin arrived, a greenhorn.
Beautiful as gold she was,
Cheeks red as oranges,
Tiny feet, just made for dancing.

Herelakh vi zaydn-veb gelokte
Tseyndelekh vi perelakh getokte
Eygelakh vi himl-bloy in friling
Lipelekh vi karshelekh a tsviling.

Her hair was as a silk web,
Her teeth as pearls on a string,
Her eyes, blue as skies in spring,
Her lips, just like twin cherries.

Nisht gegangen is zi, nor geshprungen,
Nisht geredt hot zi nor gezungen
Lebedik un freilech yede mine
Ot aza geven is main kuzine!

She did not walk, she leapt.
She did not talk, she sang.
Her every feature joyful and gay –
Such a one was my cousin!

Un azoy ariber tseyner yorn
Fun mayn kuzine iz a tel gevorn
'Peides' hot zi vokhenlang geklibn

Biz fun ir iz gornisht nit geblibn.

But, as the years passed by
My cousin went downhill
From working hard week after
    week.
Nothing remained but a wreck.

Haynt az ikh bagegen mayn kuzine
Un ikh freg ir: S'makhtsu epes, Grine?

Ziftst zi op, un kh'leyen in ir mine:
Brenen zol Colombus' es medine!

Today, as I meet her on the street,
And I ask: How's everything,
    Greenhorn?
She just sighs and I read in her eye:
To hell with Columbus's paradise!

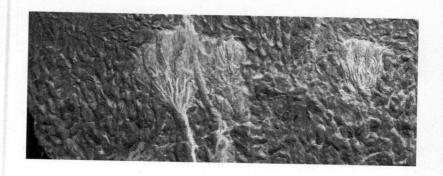

Tahar Bekri
'Epic of the thyme of Palestine'
Translated by Marilyn Hacker

Tahar Bekri, who was born in 1951 in Gabès, Tunisia, is a poet who writes both in French and in Arabic. He has lived in Paris since 1976, and has published over twenty books: poetry, memoir, essays and art books. He teaches at the Université Paris X. His most recent books include *Les dits du fleuve* (Al Manar, Paris, 2009), *Le Livre du souvenir*, (Elyzad, Tunis, 2007) and *Salam à Gaza*, to be published by Elyzad in this year. His website is tahar.bekri.free.fr.

Epic of the thyme of Palestine
In memory of Mahmoud Darwish

I perfumed the hills and plains
Nourished by brilliant light
Accompanied wanderers' steps
Through the earth's ancestral rites
All those domes, bell-towers, temples
Offered up for a thousand prayers

That sudden rain which mingled
My scent with the steadfast stones
Alert for gaping rifts
The rocks grasp leaves that I dropped
In the dusk of centuries stretching
Themselves out in history's pit

Neighbour sea, I loved your murmur
That consoled my trembling, joined
By flutes, rocked by solar olive trees
They came by night with reptilian tanks
Razored treads sheared my sprigs
That held a dream built like a stream

I still see you, children scorched by phosphorus
Ashes blackened by clouds bleached
Of blood and cowardly dust
Beneath skies gashed by cast lead
Hospitals bled from a hundred shells
Schools that are like graveyards

And I don't forget the path the wind took
To extinguish your genie-less lamps
Who could claim that a rifle was hidden
In flour, or rockets in kitchens
When beds were ripped open on sleeping
Bodies, thresholds smirched with shame

How not to see you, bats
In the blindness of the night
Master boots that march on my summers
Scoured of secular lemon-trees
How not to know you, crows
In the brainless drones overhead

Winter covered by wailing sirens
Houses like graves without stones
Among the dark cries, among ruins
I consoled the stars brusquely awakened
Terrified by your gunpowder trails
My new leaves your arsonists' martyrs

I tell you this, thyme is to flavour
Olive-oil bread kneaded and baked
On my flames, not to light your fires
Neither rosemary, friend of my cypresses
Nor waters wrenched from their source
Will pardon your memory's gaps

I tell you this, thyme is for proud
Old roads, it is not for vultures
Thyme is for birds at rest
Freed from their need and their fear
Not to starve out trees and nests
Not to punish mothers and cradles

I defy you, hyenas in helmets
Thyme, even hemmed in by the Wall
Will burst through sea, sky and earth
So many armies for one herb
Still cannot prevent my bestowing
My fragrance on open-armed people

27 January 2009

Sappho, 'Fragment 96'
Translated by Will Heath

. . . Now she bides in distant Sardis,
But often turns her thoughts
Our way, not knowing what to do.

You were a goddess in her eyes,
She prized your songs above
All else, they filled her with such joy.

Now coy Lydian women gaze,
At day's end, as she shines.
Just as the rosy-fingered moon

Soon surpasses all of the stars,
Shining far over the
Salt sea and the fields in flower,

Bowers bloom in a falling dew,
Many-hued melilot
And cloves blossoming with the rose.

Often those days return to her,
As the sun goes sinking
Down, and her heart breaks for Atthis,

But this wish to go cannot be,
So we cry songs across
The sea and flowers in between . . .

Note

There have been many attempts to render Ancient Greek verse into English by creating a corresponding metrical scheme which converts the Greek long syllables into stressed, and the short into unstressed. Some of the results have been interesting poetry in their own right, but have captured little of the quality of the originals.

A different approach may be seen in the translation above, where I have concentrated upon reproducing the phonetic features most central to the poetic effect. For example the lines 'rosy-fingered moon/ soon surpasses' echo the enjambment of the Greek 'brododaktulos Selanna/ Panta perrechoisa' and the line ending 'blossoming with the rose' recreates the last long vowel of the Greek 'melilotos anthemodes' and subsequent lingering pause, though I am of course placing the blooming roses last in the list of flowers, where they are first in the Greek.

I have not indicated my conjectures in the first and last stanzas with brackets, as they will be apparent to readers familiar with this famous poem, as will my paraphrases, all of which have been made in an attempt to render something of the music of what is, in my opinion, Sappho's masterpiece.

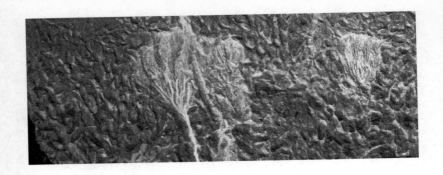

Roger Moulson
Six translations from *The Greek Anthology*

These are translations from *The Greek Anthology*, a collection of poems, mostly epigrams, that cover the classical and Byzantine periods of Greek writing. The earliest known anthology was compiled by Meleager of Gadara under the title *Anthologia* or 'Garland'. Meleager's anthology attracted later additions. The definitive edition was made by Constantine Cephalas in the tenth century AD who added a number of other collections. In many cases the dates of the poets whose work is included are not known.

I have called these poems collectively 'The Olive Oil Lamp' as that is the figure that connects the different lovers, the lamp acting as witness and confidant. In the Meleager poem the figure of the vows flowing past like water finds an echo in Keats's epitaph 'Here lies one whose name was writ in water', although Keats based it on a Beaumont and Fletcher play of 1611, *Love Lies A-Bleeding*, which says 'All your better deeds/ Shall be in water writ.' Philaenis in the third poem is the name of a servant but the other named persons are all lovers. My translations are based as closely on the texts as I could manage whilst retaining the precisely numbered syllabic structure of the originals.

The Olive Oil Lamp

1

Cleophantis is late, and now for the third time
  the lamp begins to sink and fade away.
I wish the flame in my heart would fail with the lamp,
  not keep me burning with sleepless longing.
She swore by Aphrodite she would come tonight,
  but she is not afraid of man or god.

Paulus Silentarius – 6ᵗʰ century AD

2

My heart on her heart, breast pressed to her breast,
  lips sealed by Antigone's sweet lips
and my skin as one with her skin. I'll say
  no more – let the lamp be my witness.

Marcus Argentarius – ?

3

The lamp's my confidant, Philaenis, silent on those things best
  not talked about. Make it drunk with oil!
Then leave us. For when did Love want a living witness?
  And close the door, Philaenis. Tight shut.
And you darling Xantho – and you too dear bed – it's time to learn
  the rest of Aphrodite's secrets.

Philodemus the Epicurean – 1ˢᵗ century BC

4

Sacred night and lamp, you two alone we chose
    to share the secrets of our vows.
He swore to love me, I swore I'd never leave
    and you were our joint witnesses.
Now he says those vows went by like water. Lamp,
    how can you watch him with another?

Meleager – 1st century BC

5

Dear lamp, when Heraclea was last here she swore by you
    she'd come, but hasn't. Lamp, if you're a god, please
punish the lying tart. When her boyfriend's there and they're about
    to get it on, go out and leave them in the dark.

Asclepiades – 3rd century BC

6

Why, I'm the silver lamp designed for midnight passion
    that Flaccus gave to faithless Nape
and by her bed I'm turned down low to watch the moves she makes
    just for the asking, the little cheat,
while you Flaccus cannot sleep, tormented by your thoughts,
    both of us far apart and wasting.

Statyllius Flaccus – ?

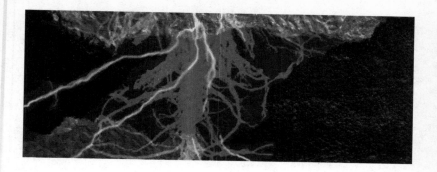

Horace, III, 30
Translated by Paul Harris

In this English version of the last poem in Book III of Horace's
Odes, I have tried to convey, as far as is possible in stressed English
verse, a sense of the metre used here by Horace (known as the
First Asclepiad). Unlike metrical verse in English, in which the
beats in a line are usually counted according to where the accent
or stress falls in any given word, classical metres are based on the
'quantity' of each syllable, i.e. whether it is considered to be long
or short. In principle, whatever metre is chosen, both the number
of syllables in a line and the disposition of long and short syllables
are fixed. For example, a line composed in the First Asclepiad is
made up of twelve syllables, with a metrical pattern as follows:
long, long, long, short, short, long // long, short, short, long, short, short.
The very last syllable of a line may be long instead of short. There
must be a break or caesura (//) between the sixth and seventh
syllable. Thus, the syllable following the break must belong to
a new word or, to put it another way, a word of more than one
syllable may not straddle the caesura.

Horace, III, 30

Exegi monumentum aere perennius
regalique situ pyramidum altius,
quod non imber edax, non Aquilo impotens
possit diruere aut innumerabilis
annorum series et fuga temporum.
non omnis moriar, multaque pars mei
vitabit Libitinam; usque ego postera
crescam laude recens, dum Capitolium
scandet cum tacita virgine pontifex.
dicar, qua violens obstrepit Aufidus
et qua pauper aquae Daunus agrestium
regnavit populorum, ex humili potens
princeps Aeolium carmen ad Italos
deduxisse modos. sume superbiam
quaesitam meritis et mihi Delphica
lauro cinge volens, Melpomene, comam.

My life's work is a book: that is my monument,
Yet more lasting than brass. Even the pyramids
Shall not match it in fame. Safe from the wasting work
Of rough winds and the rain, proof against time itself,
Countless years shall not blot me from men's memory.
Its contents shall preserve what is the better part
Of myself, with my praise destined to shine more bright,
My verse grow even more dear to posterity,
While Rome's true to her gods. There, they shall say of me,
Where swift Aufidus' stream waters a thirsty land
And King Daunus of old governed a simple folk
Whose roots lay in the soil: 'Humble his origins
Just like us, but he won fame through his poetry,
Put our place on the map; he was the first to make
Latin syllables dance timed to a Sapphic beat.'
Take pride, then, O my Muse. Take up your due reward,
Nor grudge me a deserved laurel to crown my brow.

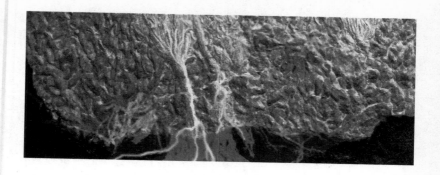

Du Fu
Three poems
Translated by Jonathan Waley

Note

The advertisement for this issue of *MPT* envisaged the problem of form in translating from one language to another. I should like to suggest a widening of the scope of this discussion, to include the question of how different poetic forms in the original language can be differentiated when they are transplanted into English.

Over the past forty years or so, translators from Chinese have tended to favour the shorter poems from periods such as the Tang dynasty (618–907 AD). I suspect that this has created a lopsided view of Chinese poetry, that it is all very short and imagistically very dense. This illusion was probably furthered by a recent interviewee on Ian Macmillan's The Verb, who claimed that 'most Chinese poetry is haiku-style'!

In fact Du Fu, like the other most famous Tang poets (such as Li Bo, Bo Juyi) wrote many longer poems which critics ancient and modern have included among his greatest. The problem of form arises here: if his longer poems are to be appreciated as distinctively different from the shorter ones, they will need to feel very different to the English reader. In particular, they will need to reflect the swiftness of thought and rhythm, the loosely-structured, spoken quality of the original. One way of avoiding these issues in the case of Du Fu, which a number of translators have adopted, is to truncate his longer poems, so that they become denser and briefer. This is especially true of his two best known long poems, which have suffered this kind of mangling. As A.C. Graham noted on the first page of his introduction to Poems of the Late T'ang , 'the element in poetry which travels best is of course concrete imagery'.

When I came to translate these longer Chinese poems, I heard them in English as lines which were generally a bit longer than an iambic pentameter; they often had a predominantly anapaestic rhythm, with about twelve syllables to the line. Perhaps it is significant that a number of very experienced readers of poetry have recognised that there was a distinctive metre, but have felt the need to ask me what it was!

These poems were written either during ('Passing Stone Niche Mountain'), or in the aftermath of, the rebellion of An Lushan (755–763 AD). This disastrous event almost toppled the Tang dynasty, and left it permanently weakened.

Passing Stone Niche Mountain
(5th Year of the Rebellion)

Bears growl near me on the left,
tigers and leopards roar off to my right,
demons shriek from behind me,
gold-tailed gibbons cry out on the path in front.
The sky has gone dark, the sun is blotted out,
mountains loom dimly, the path ahead is unclear,
as I push my cart to the base of that Stone Niche,
look up, and see a rainbow in mid-winter.

What is that bamboo-cutter up to over there,
sadly humming as he scales his cliffside ladder?

'Searching for arrow-shafts – official demands –
supplying the North-east armies five years now –
scoured these hillsides for suitable bamboo stems,
not one left that's straight enough to cull.'

What will happen when those rebel armies
burst like a howling wind on the scattering peasants?

Note
A rainbow in mid-winter: a bad omen.

Gongsun's Pupil Dances
the Sword Dance – a Ballad

An age ago, when she danced with the brilliant swords,
the ground beside us shook with her every movement.
Spectators sat there rigid, drained of colour,
whilst all around them sky and earth spun round.
Her flashing sleeves – the Archer shot nine suns down;
her proud demeanour – sky lords rode off on dragons.
She rushes on stage to the galloping beat of the drums;
she freezes – rivers are locked in glinting ice.

Her scarlet lips, pearl sleeves are just a memory,
but her art still flows through the limbs of this student of
    hers.
And here, at White Emperor City, I can again see
her student performing this dance with a thrill we all share.

When we talked together, I already had good cause;
her words took me to the depths of our recent failures.

Of his former Majesty's eight thousand entertainers,
only Gongsun could really perform the Sword-dance.
But time's sleight of hand has made fifty years flash by,
and wind-blown dust now shrouds the Imperial palace.
The Pear Garden's performers have melted like the mist,
But this ageing dancer's still bright in the winter sunlight.
Trees now lock branches on the Mound of Golden Grain,
limp grasses die on the sheer cliffs of Qutang Gorge.
And here, at the banquet, flutes rise to a pitch of joy –
till the moon shines again on the desolate aftermath.

This old man no longer knows where his feet will take him,
blistered at walking the wild hills, aghast at the pace.

Notes

The Pear Garden: a music/dance academy within the Imperial Palace.

The Mound of Golden Grain: burial place of the recently deceased 'Brilliant Emperor' Xuanzong.

Qutang: one of the famous Three Gorges of the Yangtze.

Lake Dongting: The Year Wanes

The north wind howls out the waning year,
the lake and its rivers are choked with powdery snow.
Bitter weather has frozen the fishermen's nets,
the locals are trying to shoot migrating geese.

Last year rice became costly – the armies were desperate –
this year the price plummeted, the farmers were broke.
High officials on lofty horses are stuffed with meat and wine,
the looms in peasant huts are eerily silent.
The men of the south rate fish, they won't eat bird-flesh;
please stop your pointless killing of passing geese!
The farmers are selling their children into slavery,
using the hard earnings to pay their taxes.

Officials used to seize counterfeit coins when desperate,
now pure bronze may be diluted with lead and iron.
They might as well stamp clay to make their money;
good and evil should not be mixed in this way.
On city walls all over the country bugles blow,
O when will these plaintive notes come to an end?

Miklós Radnóti
Four poems
Translated by Stephen Capus

Miklós Radnóti was born in 1909 into a Jewish family in Budapest. After graduating from Szeged University he was prevented by his ethnic background from obtaining a teaching post and was obliged to support himself as a private tutor and translator. His translations include the poems of the Roman poet Virgil which were to have an important influence on his own later work. While a student he had joined a group of left-wing intellectuals and the friendships he formed here played a significant role in the shaping of his socio-political outlook. Another decisive event during this early period was his marriage to his wife, Fanni, to whom some of his greatest poems were to be addressed.

In the early forties, having come under the influence of leading Catholic intellectuals, Radnóti formally converted to that religion. He was by this time beginning to be recognized as one of the most significant young Hungarian poets. Nonetheless, he was compelled after the outbreak of the Second World War to serve several terms of forced labour. It was during the last of these, on a forced march from Yugoslavia, that he was executed in 1944.

As is the case with most Hungarian poets writing in the first half of the 20th century, metre and rhyme are an integral part of Radnóti's poetry. This is above all the case in his later writing where formal elements play a crucial role in his efforts to articulate his experience as a Jew writing in Hungary during the World War. Here his classical prosody, including metres derived from his study of the Roman poet Virgil, are inextricably bound up with the humanistic values of the Western tradition which he defiantly affirms in the face of Hungary's accelerating descent into intolerance and violence. In his last poems, dating from the period of his labour service, the poise and harmony of his prosody, together with the scrupulously articulated semantic and syntactic structures with which they intersect, provide a counterbalance to the narrative of personal dislocation and suffering. It is by means of the formal accomplishment of these poems that Radnóti is able to impose a sense upon, and to triumph over, the chaos and horror of his experience.

However others might see this patch of earth . . .

However others might see this patch of earth
Now ravaged by flames, for me it's the place of my birth,
The little land where my childhood once arose.
I grew from this soil, like the tender branch that grows
From the trunk, and I hope I'll rest in it when I die.
This is my home. I know the trees I pass by,
I know their names, the flowers they bear, I know
The dreams of the people who hurry along the road
And I know for them on a summer evening the flames
That gush from ruined houses mean grief and pain.
This land's just a map for the man who flies through the sky,
But for me it's the place where Vörösmarthy died;
For him all it hides is the factory he means to bomb,

But to me it's the oxen, the church and the peaceful farm;
Through his sights ploughed fields and factories are all he
    can see,
But the pain of the worker is just as real to me
And the forest, too, the orchard, the graves, and among them
The old woman who quietly weeps for her vanished loved
    ones;
And what's just a railway to bomb, for me instead
Is the pointsman's house – I can see him there with a red
Flag in his hand, sending signals, his children around him
While all round the factory yard his sheepdog is bounding;
And there's the park where lost love still leave a trace
And in my mouth the memory of kisses that taste
Like honey; and walking to school, I'd pass this stone
In the kerb upon which I'd step – for it alone
Could bring me luck – but from high it remains concealed,
There's no gadget by which such things can be revealed.

Yes, we too are guilty, like other men
And we own our transgressions, the how, the where and the
    when.
But workers live here and poets who have no hand in
Our guilt, and childen awakened by understanding;
In darkened cellars they nurture its light till once more
The finger of peace inscribes its sign on our doors
And posterity answers our word and resurrects us.
Until that day, broad wing of night, protect us.

Letter to my wife

Soundless worlds are listening somewhere deep
In the earth; the silence roars in my ears and I keep
On crying for help but from Serbia stunned by war
No one can give me an answer and you are far
Away. The sound of your voice becomes entwined
With my dreams and, when I awake next day, I find
Your words in my heart; I listen and meanwhile the sound
Of tall, proud ferns, cool to the touch, murmurs all round.

When I'll see you again, I can no longer promise – you
Who once were as grave as the psalms, and as palpably true,
As lovely as light and shade and to whom I could find
My way back without eyes or ears – but now in my mind
You stray through a troubled land and from somewhere deep
Within it your flickering image is all I can keep
A hold of. Once you were real, but now you're a dream,
I tumble back into memory's depths till it seems

I'm a boy once more, wondering jealously whether
You love me and if, at the height of youth, you'll ever
Become my wife – I begin to hope once more
And, tumbling back, my wakeful state is restored
And I know you are – my wife, my friend, yet how
Far off. Beyond three savage frontiers. Now
Autumn's coming. Will it forget me here?
The vivid memory of our kisses still endures.

I believed in miracles once, but now they've fled
And squadrons of bombers slowly drone by overhead;
In the sky I saw with amazement the blue of your eyes;
But then it grew dark and the bombs in the aeroplane high
Above were longing to fall. All the same, I came through
And now I'm a prisoner. And though I've measured the true
Scale of my hopes, I'm certain I'll reach my goal;
For you I've already travelled the length of the soul,

The roads that seek distant lands; if I must, I'll contrive
To conjure myself over red-hot coals and survive
Among showers of flames – yet still I will return
To be with you one day; if I have to, I'll learn
To be tough like the bark on a tree – and now I'm soothed
By the calm of men who, achieving power, move
Through endless trials – and the knowledge that I'll pull
    through
Descends, like a wave, with the coolness of 2 x 2.

Camp Heidenau, in the hills above Zagubica, 1944.
August–September.

Sleep

Someone's always being murdered
Somewhere – while eyes are averted
In the depths of a valley, or openly
On mountain tops lit by publicity –
Anywhere you like – and you're wrong
To argue that it's happening a long
Way off from here: Shanghai
Or Guernica are as close to my
Own heart as your trembling hand or
The lofty orbit of Jupiter!
Don't look at the sky now
Nor at the ground but go
To sleep. For death is slipping
Stealthily through the glittering
Dust of the Milky Way, strewing
With silver the darkness in ruins.

Peace, dread

When I left the house it was ten o'clock,
The baker rode past, singing, too busy to stop,
Overhead droned a plane, day blazed, it was ten o'clock,
I thought of my dead brother and somewhere above
Drifted every one of the people I ever loved
But who live no more, the silent ghosts of all
My days swept past and a shadow lay on a wall.
Hush fell, it was ten oclock, the morning stopped dead,
Down the street fluttered peace and a kind of nameless
  dread.

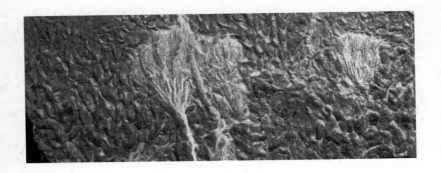

Four Afghan Poems
Translated from the Persian by Zuzanna Olszewska

The poems and translations

The Afghan poets translated here all lived for many years as
refugees in Iran and were leaders of or participants in a blossoming
Afghan literary renaissance in exile. They represent the poets'
responses to the war, occupation, poverty, and violation of human
rights that their homeland has experienced in the past three
decades, but also their sense of responsibility as intellectuals and
artists to bear witness to this reality.

The translation of blank verse (in the poem 'Peace') was
relatively straightforward, but I have tried to render in metric verse
the three other poems presented here, which are *ghazal*s or short
lyrics with a monorhyme scheme. It was difficult to reproduce
the original rhyme schemes without sacrificing the imagery, but
in the *ghazal*s here the *radif* or 'overrhyme', a word or short phrase
which is repeated immediately after the rhyming syllable, is visible
in the translations and contributes to the structural unity of the
poems. The use of iambic or trochaic heptameter for the *ghazal*s,
which proved to be the most comfortable metres, is in a sense
an impoverishment because Persian has a much greater diversity

of metres which was impossible to reproduce, but it is my hope that the rhythm will give a sense of the formal structuring of the originals. My translation of the *ghazal* by Sayed Asef Hossaini is the only one in which I have managed – serendipitously – to be completely true to the *ghazal* form, incorporating metre, rhyme and *radif,* and retaining the poem's original imagery.

The poets

Sayed AbuTaleb Mozaffari was born in Oruzgan province in Afghanistan in 1965. He moved to Iran, where he studied in a Shi'a seminary in Mashhad. He was one of the founding members and is currently director of the Dorr-e Dari ('Pearl of the Dari Language') Cultural Institute for Afghan refugees in Mashhad. He has published five volumes of his own poetry or edited collections of others', and is the managing editor of *Khat-e Sevvom*, a quarterly cultural and literary journal.

Mahboubeh Ebrahimi was born in Kandahar in 1977 and obtained a degree in Public Health from Tehran University while organising Afghan cultural events in Tehran. She now lives in Kabul with her poet husband and three children. She has published one volume of poetry, *Badha khaharan-e man and* (The Winds are my Sisters, 2007).

Sayed Asef Hossaini was born in Mazar-e Sharif in 1980 and grew up in Mashhad. He later studied at Kabul University and at Erfurt University in Germany. He has published two volumes of poetry, *Man dar asar-e mah-gereftegi* (I, Born of the Lunar Eclipse) and *In kafshha-ye piadeh* (These Walking Shoes).

Bakht-Avar

By Sayed AbuTaleb Mozaffari

Bakht-Avar has come to stand behind the glass, freezing.
We are sitting on this side, our blood and bones freezing.
Her two green eyes seem to implore: Diners, would you
    mind,
could I have a morsel of your food, please, I'm freezing?
With her anxious glances she awaits the moment when
'Mister' stumbles out, in stylish dress, stoned, and freezing.
Here a leery group from seven corners of the earth,
bulging pockets head towards the till to pay, freezing;
there a train of beggar brides awaits in ragged clothes,
tens of girls like Bakht-Avar that ply their trade, freezing.
Here a poet sits, a glass of tea held in his palm,
In his fist a poem, in his head his thoughts freezing.

Herat Restaurant, Kabul, Winter 2001

(Note: Bakht-Avar is an Afghan girl's name, meaning one who
brings good luck.)

Morning, News of War
By Mahboubeh Ebrahimi

Today the television sets showed you once again
and shook the morning of contented people once again.
You, the blackest hole of man's existence on this earth
were shown to all the carefree people of the world again.
It didn't matter how the morning started out for you
or why your birds were dying by the score, by the score.
The angels standing guard upon the shoulders of the earth
taught the children how to fly to heaven once again.
Once again a world of hearts briefly bled for you —
today the television sets showed you once again.

Tehran, Iran, November 2001

Peace
By Mahboubeh Ebrahimi

A rifle on your shoulder
you come out to greet me,
dishevelled, dressed in rags.
This
is not you.
You were supposed to be
a rider on a red horse...

Upon my hair you place
a crown of poppy blossoms –
Roses?
You smile
and half-dead butterflies
fall to the dust.
Release me!
I'm afraid of you.
You've hidden minefields in your pockets.
They've killed people
and thrown them into the wells of your heart.

Your kisses say –
But your voice,
tired and hoarse, reaches me
– Come, let's go home.
If you kiss me,
the mines will be disarmed,
the guns,
the poppies.
Your kiss
is a white dove
with a delicate flower in its beak.

2004

Ghazal
By Sayed Asef Hossaini

You don't need to feel obliged to stay with me, my love,
to put up with my miseries so patiently, my love.
I am prepared to live with hate and fear of blowing up;
but you, a delicate crystal cup – how could you be, my love?
Actually, for two days now I've struggled with the thought
that I should mutely ask you with all honesty, my love:
How could you ever fit into this hamlet, bare and cold,
when you're a city, a vast world, a galaxy, my love?
Set aflame this forest facing its last bitter days
so that one day my phoenix might take wing: be free, my
    love!
O my unbelieving poem, O fruitless time, I'm just
an uncompleted letter resting on your knee, my love.

This leprous age has gnawed away my face, yet even so
your petals dance upon my eyelids heedlessly, my love .

Kabul, 2007

Amina Saïd
Two poems
Translated by Marilyn Hacker

Amina Saïd was born in 1953 to a Tunisian father and a French
mother, in Tunis, Tunisia. She began writing poetry in French
at a young age. After her studies in English Literature at the
Sorbonne, she briefly taught at the Faculty of the Arts in Tunis
before settling in Paris, making frequent trips to her homeland.
She then turned towards journalism. A meeting with the Filipino
writer, F. Sionil José, led to her translations of several of his short
stories and novels from the English. She has since published
thirteen collections of poetry, which include *La Douleur des seuils*
(2002), *Au présent du monde* (2006) and *L' Absence l'inachevé* (2009)
— published by Éditions de la Différence — as well as *Tombeau
pour sept frères*, with calligraphy by Hassan Massoudy (Éditions
Al Manar, 2008). Her additional work includes two collections
of tales from Tunisia. More than most contemporary poets, there
is a characteristic vocabulary associated with her work, like an
underlying sketch: the sky and its silence, the sea, light, the human
eye, stone, exile: an impossible eternal return to a landscape of
childhood. But she has also presented her work at innumerable
international festivals, and the idea of certain human verities, not
all pleasant ones, remaining constant as the scenery and language
change, is also a preoccupation.

Durban seaport at night

on the white boat
is my friend Chirikure
with an Amstel in each hand
Vusi sings times are
good when we meet
welcome to South
Africa welcome
I ask Ilja where I am
the Zulu poet Gladman
drives us down roads
              of words
I find the Indian Ocean again
a peeled drum the sun
sets on our dreams
              I go off
down the rectilinear streets
North Street East Street
West Street Durban blues
Smith Street Bottle Shop
alcohol is sold behind
iron barriers
Durban blues
you're smiled at
you're assaulted
someone puts out a hand
for a few rands
welcome to South
Africa welcome
the Zulu warriors
keep watch for nightfall
at dawn they dance
for the tourists
a peeled drum the sun

overcomes our nightmares
the mammas snooze
behind their market stalls
masks masks masks
large gray birds
probe the lawns
coconut trees preen the sky
          I go off
down the rectilinear streets
Palmer Street Mile Street
Hunter Street Durban blues
Victoria Street Market
knives saris tripe
fish tobacco guavas spices
masks masks masks
welcome to this mixed-up
country welcome
this country Antjie my friend
this country is also
sorrowfully yours
townships shacks shacks shacks
make this country
a livable place
Botha's Hills Thousand Hills
round houses sugar cane
cows with solar horns
little leaping monkeys
nameless hamlets
the Zulu warriors
have put away their spears
women's breasts
bounce beneath
an abundance of pearls
sing Vusi sing
ma mayibuye i Afrika
welcome to KwaZulu-

Natal welcome
we have talked
in the shade of the marula
we read poem after poem
Sheri-D my friend yes
we are drunk with wine
with words while I read I dance
I make love to the words
silence shatters
in diamond shards
I am a poem poem poem
which dies in my mouth
you haven't seen anything in Durban
Durban blues Jo'burg blues
we read poem after poem
Vusi sings times are bad when separation
keeps worming its way in
remember remember
what you forgot
to see in Durban

cove of Durban's port

where the lights of the city are dancing
the trees' silence within eternal summer the ocean's silence
from which a new day is hoisted each morning
silence on the lawns where gray birds graze
silence of the poet arm slashed by a rusty blade
parodies of masks turned toward the silent sky
citizens drunk on beer as soon as night's curtain
falls each one barricaded in silence
because too many words remain unsayable
those words that Sandile shrieked on stage and elsewhere
as the rusty blade shrieked through the poet's arm

shacks on the outskirts abandoned villages within
women in flowered dresses waiting for the improbable
curious little monkeys by the roadsides
a stop beneath the heady marula the liquor tree
all at once I speak of a voyage to the heart of another desert

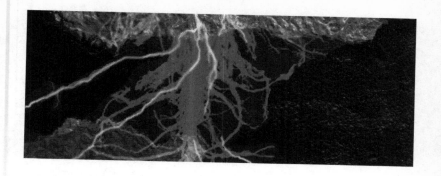

Alejandra Pizarnik
Poems
Translated by Cecilia Rossi

Alejandra Pizarnik was born in Avellaneda, a suburb to the south of Buenos Aires, in 1936. As the daughter of Russian Jewish immigrants, Yiddish was the language spoken to her at home throughout her childhood and learnt at the Zalman Reizien Schule in Avellaneda. Later on, she was to reject her mother tongue to adopt Spanish, a language in which her voice would always sound foreign. Her friend and poet Ivonne Bordelois recalls this:

> Alejandra literally spoke from the other side of language and in every language, including Spanish, and above all in Spanish, one would hear her speaking within a hallucinatory schizophrenia. . . . the rhythm of her words broken up in unpredictable places, 'soth-at-you-seethep-o-em', produced a certain hypnotism, similar to that which inspires us to look at old photographs in which we do recognise features, but which are in every way as unexpected as they are oblique.

Thus, there is the sense that poetry for Pizarnik is essentially a mode of translation: 'some traversal *outside* yourself, away from *home*, venturing toward the language of the other in view of an impossible or denied translation,' as Derrida says. Her desired language, 'of the other', i.e. the poetic language, was something she sought for, and found as she made the 'body of the poem with her body'. As I was finalising the translation of Pizarnik's *Poesía completa* I wrote in my translator's journal words which encapsulate this process of becoming in language:

> The desire to live in the phrase: the phrase like a body, which she embraces and which embraces her. It replaces, or displaces love. Not only does she live in language, but she is made in it, by it. Examining this process of becoming the poem — body and soul — of being on the page, in the words, until you begin to see how they have captured your breath so the words breathe you, effectively *live* you (subject turned object: the nominative displaced by the accusative) I am reminded of this definition of 'syntax' by Eavan Boland in a poem called 'Lava Cameo': 'a structure extrinsic to meaning which uncovers the inner secret of it'. Where the extrinsic and the intrinsic merge, like body and soul, poem and page, is in the reading and the writing. Hence, in translation.

For this reason, the metaphor of *transplant* with its meaning of transferring an organ or organs from one body to another is most apt to talk about the process of translating a poetry that is, above all, conceived of as 'body'. Even in her diaries Pizarnik wrote about this relationship body-language. If she did the *relaxe* exercises intended to help her distend her throat, so that she could breathe harmoniously, then her relationship with language would change: she would speak the literary language (entry on 1 December 1963). The task of the Pizarnik translator is, then, concerned with remaking Pizarnik's voice in English so that the body of her poem lives on.

No Land in Common

Sometime you'll know why you speak less than you say. Sometime you'll find what you'd already said you said. You alone can speak of speaking because it is your emblem, your scourge.

Even now, also now, hostile syllables clash in your body. But you know one day they'll be set free, burst in, and you'll never say the words of everyone, those which refuse to serve you, because they're not right for you

Small Poems in Prose

The sun closed down, the sense of the sun closed down, the sense of closing was illumined.

*

A day comes when poetry is made without language, the day when the big and small desires spread out across verses are summoned, suddenly gathered in two eyes, the same I have praised so much in the frenzied absence of the blank page.

*

Enamoured of the words that make small nights in what's unmade of the day and its fierce void.
*

Silent and Blue on the Edge of the Swamp
To Enrique Pichon Rivière

They have closed the face that was identical to the loftiest dream from an august childhood and timorous birds in a fast flurry of black feathers made a landscape for the most perfect terror. I'm your silence, your tragedy, your mourner. Since I'm only night, since all the night of my life is yours.

In the Open Darkness

If the smallest death demands a song I must sing to those who were lilacs who silenced their fires to accompany me in my black light when a shadow formed by my lament sheltered in their shadows.

She the Obscure

And why did I talk as if silence were a wall and words the colours destined to cover it? And who said it feeds on music and cannot weep?

Painting

Sounds of somebody going up a staircase. The woman of torments, who returns from nature, climbs a staircase down which flows a trail of blood. Black birds burn the flower of distance in the hair of the solitary woman. We must save, not the flower, but the words.

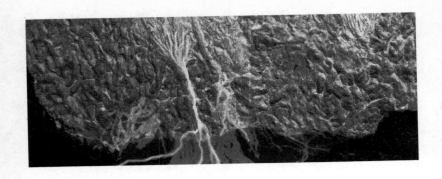

Kristiina Ehin
Seven poems
Translated by Ilmar Lehtpere

Kristiina Ehin was born in Rapla, Estonia in 1977. She received an M.A. in Comparative and Estonian Folklore from Tartu University in 2004. She has published five volumes of poetry in her native Estonia and has won a number of prizes there, including Estonia's most prestigious poetry prize for her fourth volume, written during a year spent as a nature reserve warden on an uninhabited island off Estonia's north coast. She has also published a book of short stories and has written a play as well. *The Drums of Silence* (Oleander Press, Cambridge, 2007), a volume of her selected poems in English translation, was awarded the Poetry Society Corneliu M. Popescu Prize for European Poetry in Translation in 2007. Her other books in English translation are *The Scent of Your Shadow*, a new collection of poetry due to be published by Arc in 2010 (with a PBS Recommendation), *Põletades pimedust – Burning the Darkness – An Dorchadas á Dhó* (trilingual Estonian-English-Irish selected poems, Coiscéim, Dublin, 2009), *A Priceless Nest* (short stories, Oleander Press, 2009), *Päevaseiskaja – South-Estonian Fairy Tales* (Huma, Tallinn, 2009) and *Noorkuuhommik – New Moon Morning* (selected poems, Huma, 2007). Work has begun on a new trilingual Estonian-English-Scottish Gaelic volume of her poems. She is often invited

to take part in international arts and literary festivals and her
poetry and prose appear regularly in English translation in
leading Irish and British literary journals. Her work has been
translated into twelve languages.

With the coming of dusk . . .

With the coming of dusk
and the dropping of leaves I become
more and more nocturnal
I am brimming
with this summer evening's nameless hum

I become ever more nocturnal
and I don't need your fire today
the fire of the coals of your feelings
to warm myself

Together with the dusk I become
more like the white lilac
forget-me-not blue
lupin purple
ever more summer-night nocturnal
more nocturnal than this rainless Seven Brothers' Day night
I fall ever deeper into the lap of night
between the back garden's nettle bushes

I don't need your fire today
today I embrace
the big pure moon
to warm myself
I become more and more evening
ever more boat-like
more girlish and young-mannish
more blue-eyed
and milky
in this garden which is full
of foaming waves of white clover
and the hooting of young owls

I become ever more thirsty
and from this thirst my thirst is fulfilled
I become ever more serious
become the truth of this night
ever darker
more delightful
the sister
of this Seven Brothers' Day night

Cows come from the sea . . .

Cows come from the sea
on this morning at the beginning of time
blue-green cows
udders full of salty sea milk
and the Sea Mother drives them ashore
with a switch of sea-grass

Sea Maidens come keep the cows
and keep yourselves
from lecherous herders by night
In autumn may a hundred blue-green cows
be back here in the bay between mottled stones
May their horns glisten in the mist
and may your eyes sparkle
But keep your hearts clear and cool
like the morning dew

You will never get used to the life of human women
it puts fetters on the heart
dreams are never fulfilled
and feelings only give rise to grief
People are beautiful but cruel
They keep to their kin like insects
they gather the gold of dreams by night
squander it all away in the morning

To become someone's own means being
dangerously close to a human star

But your eyes are like the sea of the world
stars drown in it

Sea Maidens come keep the cows
But keep your hearts clear and cool
like the morning dew

I wait for you adventurer mad rover . . .

I wait for you adventurer mad rover
I wind yellow crêpe paper roses
round copper wire
put wood on the fire
in honour of this pitilessly cold
February day
I feel your movements
your slow strong coming
towards me
towards my world
through the snowstorm

You're already there long since
and yet you aren't
We've looked into each other's eyes
only in dreams
your eyes inside me
your mouth inside me
your heart right here
closer than anything else

I don't give you my breast any more . . .

I don't give you my breast any more
The apple trees are in blossom for the second time in your
    life
I lull you to sleep beneath our garden's
first and only Antonovka apple tree
and the juice sloshing around in your baby-bottle
is from that very same tree

Juice from the autumn before last
when we were still one
when I wasn't really a mother yet
and you weren't really a child

Here I want to be
your big sinewy
mother smelling of Antonovka
Really your mother
even though I don't give you my breast anymore
you
really my child

The smell of white horses can be felt . . .

The smell of white horses can be felt
Rainwater on the marble steps
slippery and dangerous
Figs
as ripe as my
anger against you

The cold moment of sunset
where nobody falls into
anyone's arms
Even mother and child
look alone
into the deep valley of their
dreams

A mother who is always
a full-time mother
A child who is still
utterly a child

We wake
A glowing purple streak of day
in the night sky
entices us out
I wheel the child
into the valley of the mother of God

Stars fall
into pieces on the gravel road
Lantern light makes the skirts of passers-by
flutter
Mens' eyes appear especially black

I am empty
from the beauty of the purple streak in the sky
the horses of the mother of God
and the scent of your shadow
at the bottom of the valley

I take off my bridal dress . . .

I take off my bridal dress
for the first and last time

Night in my fingers on my back
Rain thrashing
against the balcony
In the park lustful peacocks calling

      quaaack-quaaack

I get the snaps undone
and slide the zip down
And already the silk slips down
over my waist stomach and legs
falls rustling onto the floor
again the birds call
again the cocks cry

      quaaack-quaaack

I open the airing window fire window and water window
roof window and cellar window
outside door and inside door
and slip into new many-coloured feathered raiment
unfurl my tail
and gather into myself all of this night's passion
sorrow and rain

I will never become a blushing
one-dimensional bride
on this pagan night
I remain regardless
of the white dress
custom and law
the bearer of feathered hominids into the world

The garden is full . . .

The garden is full
of the song of my white feet

My soul is like these threads of spider silk
tensed
criss-cross
between two apple trees

Before dawn
bodies are heavy
sleep presses eyelids down
You sleep
eyelashes resting on your cheeks
morning has not yet touched the fields of your dreams
the lonely open land of your subconscious

Sleep-sleep
your arms around me
Here the night is safe and sound
The garden is criss-cross full
of spider silk
and the song of my white feet

Note

An exile, transplanted into a foreign society, strives at all costs
to retain his or her identity. A translated poem is, in a sense,
also an exile, transplanted into the alien environment of a foreign
language. One of the translator's many tasks is to be sensitive and
welcoming, helping the poem retain its identity and adapt to its
new environment without making compromises. To this end my
bilingual upbringing as the child of Estonian refugees has been

an enormous benefit, giving me a native speaker's understanding of the cultural and linguistic nuances of both Estonian and English.

I have been translating Kristiina Ehin's poetry, prose and drama for nearly five years and have translated nearly all of her published work along with much of her as yet unpublished work as well. Working so intensively with the work of the poet I admire most in any language, I have gained a deep understanding of her work and an increasingly clear insight into the complexity of the translation process. It goes far beyond linguistic competence and is in itself an act of creativity.

At the heart of this process is the author's voice with its own particular music, its idiosyncracies and nuances. When I translate Kristiina's work, I hear her voice reading what I have written. The music of her voice dictates the music of my translation. Her imagery is sometimes very specifically Estonian, but I trust in the reader's wish to experience what is Estonian in Kristiina's work, and I don't look for British equivalents. My translations strive to be Kristiina's poems, not my interpretations of them.

The most important factor for me in transplanting Kristiina's poems into the soil of the English language continues to be a deep inner need to see them thrive there in their own right as they do at home in the Estonian language.

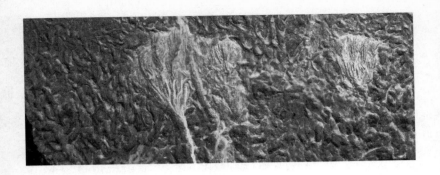

Francis Combes
Four poems
Translated by Alan Dent

Francis Combes has published fifteen books of poetry, including *La Fabrique du bonheur, Cause commune, Le Carnet bleu de chine* and *La Clef du monde est dans l'entrée à gauche.* He has translated several poets into French, including Heine, Brecht, Mayakovsky and Attila Joszef. He has also published two novels and, with his wife Patricia Latour, *Conversation avec Henri Lefebvre.* He is a founder of the radical publishing cooperative, Le Temps des Cerises, and was for many years responsible for putting poems on the Paris Metro.

Eulogy and condemnation of work

Are you strong enough to sing of the inhuman work of men ?
Man's achievements, his passing contradictions,
    the ever more complex construction of his honeycombed palaces
in his kingdom of the bees ?
Have you the heart to sing of the heartless law of men
whose every new conquest is paid for
by a new mutilation ?
Will you find the words to dispel the ancient curse ?
For thousands of years we have advanced like a procession of
    dockhands, to erect new pyramids.
We raise into the sky cathedral arches where only
    our fantasies can live,
We build blind, black crystal towers,
which admit into their heads buzzing with missiles
    nothing but the murderous swarm of figures
from the Stock Exchange and world trade.
We are capable of miracles in the midst of horror.
We do our best to make our home
    uninhabitable.
And yet
we are also carpenters,
our hands good and precise with the wood,
we've always known how to build,
and we know, once the white roof-frame on the school's done
how to tie a bouquet of wild roses.
Peasant, chemist, metal-worker, pilot or computer expert,
we know the measure and the secret weight of things,
we organise metamorphoses,
master the dancing curve of the universe.
We could make this earth a home.

The world of divided men

Born from the division of labour
the system feeds on the division of men
from one another
and the division they maintain, engender and multiply
within themselves.
So we live in the age of divided men
the age of division
of work and of richness
of production and exchange
of progress and modernity
of the heart and of reason
of the body and the mind
of science and the dream
of the useful and the beautiful
of art and life
of morality and politics
because the division of labour
which never stops perfecting itself as it moves
is the condition of efficiency
and the reason for absurdity.

The achievements of capitalism

So this system will have achieved miracles before our very
    eyes:
under its reign abundance reveals itself the cause of poverty,
progress engenders barbarism,
the strengthening of the State, insecurity

the development of media
under-information
the scintillating conquests of science
generalised ignorance
economic globalisation
tribal wars
the unification of the world market
the division of workers and peoples,
as for artists
all that remains for them
is to produce commodities
and to cultivate ugliness.

The ages of humanity

According to Hesiod, humanity passed through several ages:
The Golden Age
when humans still lived
in the company of innocent
beautiful and happy gods;
The Silver Age, during which the decline began,
The Bronze Age, still primitive,
and finally The Iron Age
(the dark and violent time
in which he lived).
Since then,
historians
archaeologists
palaeontologists
have established a different order
according to which
humanity didn't fall but ascended.

Thus, everyone knows that after the stone age
came the bronze age
then the iron age
which preceded ours.
The question we should be asking now is:
When will we finally leave behind the age of money?

Blanca Varela
Four poems
Translated by Ruth Fainlight

Born in Lima, Peru in 1926, Blanca Varela became associated with a group of intellectuals, artists and writers known as the Generation of 1950. Between 1949 and 1957 she lived in Europe and the United States. In Paris she met the Mexican writer Octavio Paz, and later wrote: 'Through Paz ... I understood and learned that poetry is a daily task, that we don't choose it, it chooses us. We don't own it; it owns us. It's nothing more than reality and at the same time the only and true escape route from reality.' Varela published her first book of poems, *That Port Exists*, in 1959, after her return to Peru, and several more collections subsequently. She became a leading figure in Latin American poetry, and received many awards for her work, including the Federico Garcia Lorca International Poetry Prize (the first woman ever to receive it), and the Queen Sophia Prize for Ibero-American Poetry. She died in Lima in 2009.

I met Blanca Varela in Lima in 1998, at an international festival in the city. Until then, I had not read a full collection or selection of her poems, only a few in journals from the USA – but I was aware of how highly esteemed she was in Latin America, and delighted and honoured to have her as one of the two translators of the work I was going to read. During that week we spent several hours in cafés or the hotel lobby talking about our writing and our lives, and when I returned a year later to a conference of women writers at the University of Lima, we met again. From then on we kept in touch — mostly by letter or the occasional telephone call. (This was before email!) We sent each other many of our books — new ones as they appeared, as well as earlier publications. There was much in *Canto Villano*, a selection from her books published between 1949 and 1994, which excited me with the desire to translate, transform and transplant these poems into my own language. I saw the process as being like carefully loosening and lifting a plant from the earth where it grew to move into another garden, making sure that even the finest tendrils of root were not broken or damaged — for if this were to happen, the plant would not take hold and flourish in its new home. When I explained this to Blanca, she understood immediately.

Exercises

1
A poem
like a great battle
the poem flings me into
against no enemy except myself

I —
and the great great wind of words

2
the cloud lies
the light lies
the eyes
eternally deceived
never tire of so many lies

3
obstinate blue
unaware of being in another iris
like god in the void

4
I think of wings of music of fire
but no
that's not what I fear
only the grim justice of light

Valses y Otras Falsas Confesiones, 1964–1971

Family secret

I dreamed of a dog
of a flayed dog
its body sang its red body whined
I asked the other
the one who turns off the butcher's light
what has happened
why we are in darkness

it is a dream you are alone
there is no one else
light does not exist
you are the dog you are the barking flower
gently you sharpen your tongue
your lolling black four-legged tongue

human skin is parched by dreams
which waste and scorch
only the red canine pulp is clean
the true light lives in its gummy eyes
you are the dog
you are the flayed canine of every night
to dream of oneself is enough.

Valses y Otras Falsas Confesiones, 1964–1971

No date
to Kafka

Reasons enough, reasons enough to place first one foot and
     then the other.
Under them, neither larger than they are nor smaller, the
     inevitable shadow that advances and vaults the corner,
     doubtfully.

Reasons enough, reasons enough to stop moving, stop
     falling, stop flying.
Enough reasons to stare out the window, to watch one hand
     furtively count the fingers of the other.

Powerful reasons for before and after. Powerful reasons
   during.
The mildewed razor is the limit.
'Lasciate ogni speranza voi ch'entrate.'
One does not return from anywhere. And the twisted rule
   confirms this above the smooth air, flat as a corpse.
And there are others.
Pallor, shock, a slight nausea.
Mysterious, obscene croak from the belly singing who
   knows what.
The full body of light, like a door slamming. Inside and
   outside.
   You don't know where.

And the rest. Do they exist?

Infinite doubt. Proven suspicion.
Let yourself be dragged against the current, like a dog.
Learn to walk the rotten beam.
On the tips of your feet. On their own shadow.
Neither larger nor smaller than they are.
One, two, one, two, one, two, one.

One behind, one in front.
Against the wall, face down, in a corner.
Trembling, with a livid brilliance under your feet, neither
   larger nor smaller than they are.
Maybe, maybe the stagnant eternity which some innocent soul
   confounds with its own excrement.

Dank reasons at the mouth of the tunnel.
And the exit.
In the long run, as many reasons as necks exist.

Defend yourself from the fire with an axe. From the devil with
   an axe, from god with an axe.
From spirit and flesh with an axe.
There will be no witnesses.
We have been warned that the heavens are dumb.

At most it will be written, will be deleted. Will be forgotten.
And already there will not be enough reasons to go back to
      place
   one foot and then the other.
Nevertheless, beneath them, neither larger nor smaller than
   they are, the inevitable shadow will be advancing.
And will vault the same corner. Doubtfully.

                           Ejercicios Materiales, 1978–1993

Final scene

I have left the door ajar
I am an animal who won't accept it has to die

eternity is the dark hinge that yields
a small noise in the night of the flesh

I am the island that moves forward fed by death
or a city savagely besieged by life

or maybe I'm nothing
only insomnia
and the brilliant indifference of stars

desert destiny
inexorably the sun of the living rises
I acknowledge this door
there is no other

untimely spring ice
and a thorn of blood
in the rose's eye

Ejercicios Materiales, 1978–1993

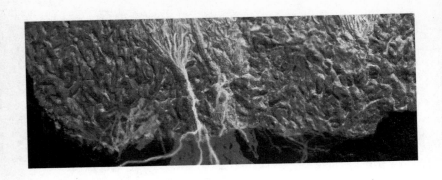

Amelia Rosselli
Extracts from *Variazioni belliche*
Translated by Cristina Viti

Born in Paris in 1930, Amelia Rosselli was seven when her father
and uncle, exiled leaders of the Italian Resistance, were murdered
by Fascist killers. After the Nazi invasion of France, Rosselli's
English mother fled with her family first to England, then to
Larchmont, NY (where Fermi, Toscanini and Salvemini, a family
friend, had also been directed by the Mazzini Society). At sixteen,
after a brief period in Florence, Rosselli returned to England on
account of her academic qualifications not being recognized in
Italy, and began the study of music while finishing high school in
London and acquainting herself with English labourism. In 1948
she moved back to Italy and began to work as a translator, despite
suffering her first nervous breakdown following the death of her
mother. Between 1952 and 1960 she published several important
essays on acoustics and ethnomusicology.

In 1950, at the Resistance congress in Venice, she met Rocco
Scotellaro (see *MPT* 3/10) and Carlo Levi. The beginning of the
deep friendship with Scotellaro, which lasted until he died, aged
thirty, three years later, coincided with Rosselli's beginnings as a
poet, though it was his politically engaged prose (and especially
the unfinished reportage *Contadini del sud*) that Rosselli felt and
openly acknowledged as a direct influence – perhaps because

it confirmed her sense of the practice of writing as a political activity that carries precise responsibilities (first and foremost the duty to remain silent rather than indulging in populism or irrelevance).

At twenty-nine Rosselli renounced the formal music studies that had taken her to Darmstadt and Paris, to give total attention to writing, living alone as a rank and file member of the Communist Party in Christian-Democrat Italy, fighting isolation, breakdowns and their associated catalogue of invasive treatments on the income of a poet unaffiliated to any academic institution, impatient of 'neoavanguardia' polemics and disdainful of drawing-room tactics.

Rosselli pursued the strategy of research to uncompromising extremes; and just as her highly trained ear could perceive several of the formants in a sound spectrum, so her astonishing command of Italian, French and English gave her an uncannily acute awareness of the multiple semantic possibilities implicit in any one word. Her ability to write poetry that plays with these elements in a highly structured fashion was developed in equal measure from her early studies and from a full understanding of the modernist breakthrough in Italian poetry. In this sense, it seems to me, her numerous and explicit references to modern poets, especially Campana (whose work Montale famously defined as 'poesia in fuga', where 'fuga' is both 'flight' and 'fugue') can be considered not merely as well-known themes within which variations are to be invented – that is, found – but as premises from which to derive the heightened awareness of context that might be seen as the hallmark of postmodernism.

Rosselli's exposure of personal dilemmas is never any less than unsparing; yet her poetry reads not like the record of a therapy session, but rather like the log book of a sharp, compassionate intelligence waging war on complacency as it tries to understand the patterns underlying human behaviour and to transcribe its findings – in musical notation.

Fourteen years have passed since Rosselli, aged sixty-six, leapt to her death from the balcony of her loft in Rome; much of

her work, including critical essays, reviews and articles, is only
beginning to receive due attention.

This selection is taken from *Variazioni belliche*, the first of
the five collections published in her lifetime, part of which was
introduced by Pasolini in the review *Menabò* in 1964.

*

If in the night any doubt arose as to the essence of my
Christianity, it vanished with the cheap rock'n'roll tear
from the nearby bar. If from the night doubt arose out
of the changing disproportionate ethmosphere, then I
requested help. If in the dead-night hell I now call to me
the angels and protecting ladies who set sail for shores
vastly more direct than mine, if from free-flowing tears
I aimed missiles and unconscious ass-kickings to friends
misplaying their part as love soldiers, if the refinements
of my spirit birthed battles and contradictions, –
then boredom died inside me, mirth deranging my
unsatisfied malaise; the fine air continued and songs
unfolded feverish activities all around, street corner
shanties at sea, last tears of christ who'd not stir for
such a trifling thynge, small spell of night in my captivity.

*

For the cantatas unfolding in the air I still rhymed
fully. For the vulture that was your sinister
figure I was resolved to fight. For the poor and
the sick of mind folding their sinister figures
all through the sick streets I still sang tarantella
all along your shirt's the finest of all street songs.
Through the streets smelling like petrol we
searched the neighbour's eye for the favourite
song. For that heart of yours that I vastly prefer
to any other storm I go amiably singing some
songs not meant for your chaste ear, a banned

singer's. For the ban that stops us going on
perhaps I will lose you again and again — until the
tides of good and evil and of all the lies covering
this whole wide world have ended their catcalling.

*

We count endless corpses. We are the last human species.
We are the corpse floating putrefied on its own passion!
Calm did not nourish me the Leo sun was my desire.
My pious desire was to win the battle, overcome evil,
sadness, lies, recklessness, the plurality
of evils lies reckless acts administrations
of every evil, of every good, of every battle, of every duty
of every lie: cruelty apart the game reposited through
the philtre of unconsciousness. Love love you who fall and lie
supine your star is my dwelling place.

Fallen on the frontline. Goodness was a refrain
that couldn't shaft me but I was shafted by it! The line of
demarcation between the poor and the rich.

*

Among the rooms obscuring my cowardice there was one
    that
rang with echoes: it was the night. I feigned insanity and ran
    to
lift the insane up from the ground, like blown flowers. It
    wasn't
light thrashing between the crystals, it was my will
to survive! and you the brave were encouraging with a
    stealthy
handful of Geld groove & tongued into my desire for you
    who
shadowed away into infinity. I was your silly girl rhyming
in spectacles for two in her granite cell sympathetic to the

frescoes and affections of ye solitary. But you forgave and ran
   after
the anniversary of the Moon who amongst many mumblings
   lifted
the sun off its candlestick. You were not my church you were
my demon and the queenly night endured from eternity and
   left
in my throat was the taste of your forced laughter obscuring
   itself
in the yeasting of the east wind inside a gunpowder store.

Through the laughter in the throat my youth was obscured.
   You'd
lift her back up, silent as she was — into her castle of habits.
To sleep to force the demon to grab hold of the shreds of
my pity, — to sleep in a room covered with cloth and with
arabesques powerful as the cheekbone of your face.

*

But if within love I caught a glimpse of joy; if in
the dead of night starting awake I saw the sky was
a riot of angels: if from your happiness I would
suck my own; if from our eyes meeting I foresaw
disaster if in melancholy I fought the strong dragon of
desire; if for love I was turning somersaults if for your
songs I was left wide-eyed: all the better to hide the
goodness prize you did not give awake. Not all goodness
can be responded to.

*

If the fault lies with men then let God come
and call me outside his gross boundary walls
sallow as the alphabet I can't find. If the wall
is a sad story of failed conjunctions, then
let me race the fasting hares of my own tyranny
let me fast unto the coming of great glory.

If hell is a ravenous thing then I fear I'm one
of those who carry flames in their mouth and
don't live on air! But the racing wind spacing out
beyond all boundaries can also crown my dreams
with joyful dawns.

*

If you play a flute too purely in the privileged
woods of your mould-filled cave, I cannot
follow you into the stench of your habits. If
you open a door that slips ajar an instant and find
no sleeping beauty, I cannot unstitch this my habit
of sad fantasies. The monocle of your inventions is
a pale thing compared to the habit I offer you and have
unstitched for your prowess! Find again the secret made
the little shrub blossom near the door that opened with
quick ease, I'm staying in darkness watching you wash
your hands if you won't faint on the threshold of all joys.

*

If through the jitters I had for you I lost my purses
on every street corner; if through the harm I had
sought for myself from your invisible arms on every
street corner I had sought for myself the grief of
knowing you distant from me; if through discontent and
failed generosity I stretched through the night long threads
of spiderweb to your door (a gate locked with no hope
except for some bright idea that could not arise in my brain)
if through your restraint and my impatience I sealed all the
scrolls of control; if through my uncertainties in the middle
of a sweet and enclosed irony I was looking for you even in
the night of others: it was so as to better recognize you in the
turmoil of others: horses hanging in mid-air over the road
   that
does not go on.

*

The madness of love is but a carnival star shooting across the
    desert.
My corset grips me too tight.
Water is a frog fighting its own drowning.
Your sonnets ring false, contrived!
The natural is barred to me. O mankind who cripple your
    feet to
eat at the prescribed times, if air is your food
why do you destroy. We shall die in the various air, but it's
    not *vacuous* —

I seek the duration of safe certainties, but the clock, the
    number
has asphyxiated my beauty, and the harmony of number has
been winding me up beyond tolerance — the clock has
    numbers
too brief for my repose. The safe-box metal wins over
the invariable air. It's not one o'clock! it's infinity! Shout that
falls against the street with its safety-locker bricks.

I cannot forget time. Air is vain
The rules of life are more asphyxiating than my beauty.
I don't want to eat, I don't want to live — shout
that falls back into your hunger.
I can't abide smoking waiting for some beauty.
Some beauty of yours. But let what's mine in any case be
    yours . . .

My umberella of platitudes. To wash, eat, dress
without any trust. Gross gallery-playing. Necessary death,
necessary vehicle of our passions. The white-hot
turmoil of love. An act of beauty surviving all
necessity: mirror of all vanities. Careerism of young
girls in bloom.

*

The lady's brother was fasting on the cheap.
I'd taken it into my head I had to follow him. Save
yourself he cried out at me as he lay dying.
Your jacket is a brim of clothspun thread
washed in the river. The ideal is running off with childish
voices and unaware to wash his clothes in the river. The ideal
is running off childish and resolute to look for voices in
    kingdom come.
The ideal is a bourgeois product of female wealth.

*

Through a casually understood encounter I fell in love
with the most cunning man on earth. O lady teacher
who raps wood on my shaking hands, love is then
joy with desolation. Determination of my every act
was and has been and still is my cowardly cowed
cunning in love! O love most cunning man on the
earth that's immaculate with green scent your shrubs
have thickened with earth with tears with childishly
understood songs. O earth promised land you leave a
path that's snake-slanted for my feet my legs my
slantwise and stained-glass soul, church
habitual.

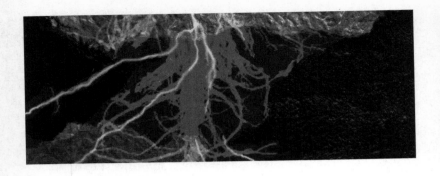

Bertolt Brecht
Ten poems
Translated by David Constantine

As in *MPT* 3/11 and 3/12 these are poems which are not readily, or at all, available in English. They are not in *Poems 1913–1956* nor in *Poems and Songs from the Plays* (Methuen 1976 and 1990, neither, at present, in print). All ten poems here are from 1922–26. In two or three there are signs of Brecht's increasing political engagement. In most he appears blackly funny, anarchic, much like his hero Baal in his enjoyments, sympathies and antipathies.

The poems are arranged chronologically and their location in the *Grosse kommentierte Berliner und Frankfurter Ausgabe* is given by volume and page, thus: 13,250. These translations appear by kind permission of the Brecht Estate, Suhrkamp Verlag and A & C Black.

Calendar Poem

It's true my skin's been eaten by the snow
My face is tanned red by the sun
Many have said they do not know me now
But fighting winter would change any man

He might sit quiet among the stones until
His bowed neck sprouts dry rot
The stars that shine upon him coolly still
Have no idea is he thin or fat

Indeed the stars know very little, they haven't seen
Him yet and he's already old
And the light is getting blacker, lard or lean
He sits and shivers in the sun, he's cold

And long ago alas and dearie me
He stopped cutting the nails of his black toes
He lets them grow and when they've grown you'll see
Him shed his boots and take a larger size

For a while he sat there in the sun
And spoke a sentence towards noon
Felt in the evening some joy again
Some peace was all he asked when night came down

Once waters flowed through him and animals
Vanished in him and he was never full
Whether he gobbled air or gobbled bulls
And now: feeble

13/250
1922

Thoughts of a Gramophone Owner

1904 I acquired it and I've never been sorry.
I always keep it hidden during the day.
Something for the dark hours of life, a nice piece of joinery
And the voice of Adelina Patti in it, pickled, as you might
   say.

The singer Adelina Patti died in 1911
God rest her soul, I've got her voice the way you get
Anything in life, for money, and a bit of paper saying where
   and when.
Her voice is still pretty good and will do me for a long time
   yet.

One day, I shouldn't wonder, it will sing to my grandchildren
   as well.
Adelina I called it from the start. Because
Of an occasion when, being in drink, we fell
My dear Adelina's voice is not quite what it was.

But it is remarkable and has astounded cleverer men than me
The things life brings. How far
We've come with our technology that she
In her wooden box is still singing Traviata!

In our grandparents' day such a thing would not have been
   possible.
Lots of the arts were doomed to oblivion and that was that.
We are after all further on in good as well as ill.
A machine like this means a sort of immortality, does it not?

Often George says, Tonight bring tobacco and Adelina round
    my place
I'm bad with my nerves. And there she is, the whole shebang
And sings her Traviata and he puts on his most respectable
    face.
For eighteen years, be it said, Traviata's all she's sung.

Many a time I might have bought other records, I admit
And right from the start my wife wanted something to
    shimmy to
But at the last moment I've always thought better of it:
Multum non multa's my motto and no one but Adelina would
    do.

13/262
Around 1922

In fact Adelina Patti died in 1919, at her castle Craig-y-Nos,
near Swansea. *Multum non multa*: much, not many – that is,
thoroughness not flightiness and superficiality.

Jeppe Karl

You met Jeppe Karl in Hamburg, he'd tell you, 'Lobster's the
    name'
He was a barman in the Crimea for a time
And a big shot in the South Seas
And the talk of Chicago once, for three days.
He was the man who in the Philippines
Chased by tigers up a monkey-bread tree
Smoked monkey-bread leaves as though he was where he had
    always wanted to be

Until there wasn't a leaf on a monkey-bread branch to be seen
Alas. But he shot the tigers and calmly went his ways.
He could also, when the mood took him, lift
Four teeth from a man without him noticing it
And for example out of the earthquake in Trebizond
He returned with a valuable pedigree hound.
He was related by marriage to German drovers and Japanese
    marchionesses.
Eight ships went to the bottom under him, he chatted
With sharks as you might with the herring lasses.

Jeppe Karl is buried in the Emerald Isle.

He met his end in almost tragic style:
In drink he drowned, hairy and matted
In a strongly stinking brandy vat
His last words: Everything's shit. Even dead

He looked frightful, it is said.

13/292
Around 1924.

Lion Feuchtwanger sketched a play called *Jeppe Karl*. Brecht's
poem may or may not have to do with that. He had a liking for
such wild men.

Remarkable how even the greatest pass . . .

Remarkable how even the greatest pass
And nothing's left but dust. Are but as grass.
Hardly anything is so terrible and unexplained as that.
In Altötting for example, Adults 2 Marks Only, you can view
The Catholic general Tilly in his coffin, treated, under glass
And a notice: Do not touch Tilly!
And I had it from the attendant himself side by side with me
    at the bier
And why should he tell me anything that wasn't true?
And what he said is right, undoubtedly:
A few years ago His Lordship the General still had hair.
Always gives you a shock, a thing like that.

13/296
1924/25

From 1630 till his death in 1632 Tilly was commander-in-chief
of the Imperial forces in the Thirty Years War. He is buried at
Altötting in Bavaria.

Sonnet on living badly

For seven years I've sat and broken bread
With baseness and with malice knee to knee
And so he'll not turn our scant water bad
I say to Envy, I'm not drinking, let it be.

I eat my pleasure from the common dish
And from the common cup I sup my sorrow
I know you wish for more. I say, Tomorrow.
Sooner, friend, you can't have what you wish.

Such conversation will not mend the soul.
Behind the locker I breathed into my fist
And smelled my breath: my breath smelled foul

And then I told myself, Soon you will die.
I've noticed since without much interest
How slowly our small lot of time goes by.

13/306
1925

Belongs in the context of Brecht's 'Augsburg Sonnets'.

The girl with the wooden leg

I was run over at the tender age
Of fourteen by a hackney carriage
Lucky really – it gave me a fright
And one leg they had to amputate
One leg – it didn't seem all that much to worry about
But that one leg even today gives me a lot of trouble
People don't think it quite natural
My Aunty gave me some lemonade right away
But it still ached a bit, I'm sorry to say
It was all right at first, for the novelty
First few weeks in the flats they addressed me very
    respectfully
One leg, hard to believe, I was only
Fifteen and because of that leg my face had wrinkles in
And now, just twenty, I'm one of the old women.

13/309
Around 1925

Song of a family from the Prairies

1
We had a farm on the Prairies
Horses, an automobile and fields of wheat
Things are bad here, said Billy
But in Frisco they'll be better
    And we had our daily bread on the Prairies
    A fresh wind and the moon on Saturday evenings
    And on the Prairies things weren't good enough for us

2
We had a house in San Francisco
An automobile business and new clothes
And: things are bad here, said Billy
But in Massachusetts they'll be better
    And we had food to eat in San Francisco
    Pretty clothes and jazz too on Saturday evenings
And in San Francisco things weren't good enough for us

3
We had a tent in Massachusetts
An oilfield and a drilling rig
Yet: things are bad here, said Billy
But in Chicago they'll be better
    And we had a roof over our heads in Massachusetts
    A stove and the Bible on Saturday evenings
And in Massachusetts things weren't good enough for us

4
We haven't got a room in Chicago
Not a dollar, no prospects, my God
And now: things are bad here, says Billy
But they won't be better anywhere else
    And once we had money and prospects
    Work in the week and free on Saturday evenings
And everywhere it wasn't good enough for us

13/317
Around 1925

Belongs in Brecht's unfinished play *Joe Fleischhacker* in a period
much concerned with the move into the big cities.

Sonnet: The Winner

Where there was no room for an olive tree's shadow
An unstoppable fighting among men began
All for a little patch of ground where nothing grew
Not even big enough to lay their corpses on

But one fought there quite without any cause
Like nothing in his violence, cursed by all
And when the slaughterers thought of flight at nightfall
He stood there fighting still, in no hurry to pause

Most men were dead by then and lying there
But he stood mowing everything around
Till nothing but him stood and he had won

When he left, the light was bad. Nevertheless I saw
His back and on his back he had a wound
He'll never lie upon his back again

13/320
Around 1925

Lines 3-4 allude to *Hamlet* 4.4, l. 18 and ll. 62-5.

Money

Don't be afraid of the dollar, child.
You should long for the dollar, child. (Wedekind)

I don't say, Work! – I won't lead you astray –
For human beings were not made to work.
But money, see that money comes your way.
Money is good. In the pursuit of money do not shirk.

Man hunts his fellow man with snares.
The wickedness of the world is great. Therefore
Get money in your purse for there's
Nothing the wicked world loves more.

Got money, they'll cling on you as ticks do, tight:
We'll know you then like the light of the sun.
Got none, your children must put you out of sight
And say, We do not know the man.

Got money, they look at you and know who's boss.
Got none, no one has heard of you.
Money will buy your case the star witness.
Money is truth. Got money, you're a hero.

What your woman tells you, you'd better believe it but
Don't go visiting her without money.
Without money you lose her, you're a have-not.
Without money only dumb animals will keep you company.

Man honours money. He extols money above God.
If you want to make sure your enemy
Won't rest in peace under the sod
Write this on his stone, Here lies Money.

13/332
1926

The epigraph is from a poem called 'Der Taler' by Frank
Wedekind, author of *Spring Awakening* and *Lulu*. He died in
1918. Brecht, who revered him, attended his funeral and wrote
an obituary.

Chorus of the Poor from *The Rich Man and the Poor Man*

The horror of being poor
Many have boasted they could bear it but
After a few years
Look at their faces.
Mouldering wallpaper and the smells of the privy
Bring the broad-chested men
Like bulls to their knees.
Watery vegetables
Destroy the plans that make a people strong.
Without water for a bath, without privacy and tobacco
You can't ask anything of anyone.
Public disregard
Ruins the spine.
The poor man
Is never alone. All are forever
Peering into his room. Their staring
Pierces his plate. He doesn't know where to turn.
The sky is his roof, it lets in the rain on him.
The earth shakes him off. The wind

Slights him. The night leaves him crippled. The day
Strips him naked. The money a man has
Is nothing, it will not save him but
Nothing can help a man
Who has none.

13/348
Around 1926

It seems Brecht planned such a play but nothing more is known
of it.

Reviews

Vénus Khoury-Ghata
Alphabets of Sand
Translated by Marilyn Hacker
Carcanet Press
232pp, paperback, £12.95
ISBN 978 1 85754 977 5

Although *Alphabets of Sand* draws together work from three
previous collections by the French-Lebanese writer Vénus
Khoury-Ghata, the style of the poems, which are all free verse
narratives predominantly in long, loose lines, and the thematic
preoccupations which are developed throughout this collection are
consistent enough that the poems sit together harmoniously. The
collection is composed of six sequences which engage particularly
with the themes of death, the correspondences between the
author's two languages, Arabic and French, and the questioning
of the nature of language itself.

Three languages are present in Marilyn Hacker's English
translation of these poems. Khoury-Ghata writes in French,
although Arabic is her mother tongue and she has described
Arabic as the 'original language' of her work. Khoury-Ghata's
poems are hybrid in both subject matter and style, blending
the fabulist narratives of traditional Arabic storytelling with a
European-informed surrealism and a bucolic magical realism

which recalls Marquez. The dead and the living coexist in a world of irreligious mythology from which linear time is banished, as discontinuous events are narrated and assembled in the poems like fragments of mosaic.

The collection starts with 'Widow', a surreal evocation of the process of the unnamed protagonist's grieving over the space of ten days. In a realistic domestic setting, fantastical scenarios occur: 'The first day after his death / she folded up her mirrors / put a slipcover on the spider web / then tied up the bed which was flapping its wings to take off.' The days are marked by the appearances of animals and people, intrusions of the natural world and by the strange rituals the woman undertakes: 'the sixth day after his death / she painted her face with earth / attacked the peaceful shadows of passers-by.' These rituals culminate in the mythic reappearance of the husband, surging out of his wife's palm like Persephone returning from the Underworld. His death is a journey on which he has lost the capacity for finding pleasure in his wife's 'usual words'.

The theme of death is reprised in 'The Darkened Ones', whose collective narrators are dead yet conscious, listening from under the ground to the sounds of the living and struggling to interpret what they hear: 'The city's voices come to us mangled / untangling them takes a land surveyor's skill.' This depiction of the restless dead under the city evokes the casualties of Lebanon's civil war who are still present in the collective memory of Beirut. The boundaries between death and life are blurred in this sequence: 'sheet or shroud, what's the difference' is a repeated refrain. The dead are not departed but rather a hidden, disenfranchised mass who feel prematurely shut out from the world. Death here is associated with a loss of words: 'without moving our hands, we write / the words which we lack, taken from disused books.'

In the sequence 'Words' the theme of language comes again to the fore. This exuberant exploded narrative is a fictional palaeontology of language which unites Khoury-Ghata's languages. The letters of the Roman and Arabic alphabets are given personalities in an origin myth: 'Language at that time was a straight line reserved for birds / the letter 'i' was the cleft of a female hummingbird.' From a common origin, the primeval word-creatures became separated, 'broke up into alphabets'. In a poem concerned with language, it is unfortunate that the phoneticisation of the names of the Arabic letters is awkward and creates unintentional resonances in English translation which distract the reader: '"Dad" is my mother said the earth / "Sad" is my stepmother/... "Sin" a slotted ladle'. As some Arabic letters have no direct equivalent in the Roman alphabet, the translator is in the unenviable position of choosing between several inexact attempts at phoneticisation in ordinary characters or utilising the International Phonetic Alphabet, which would sacrifice accessibility for precision. In this translation, Hacker has unfortunately chosen phoneticisations which not only spell out English words that Khoury-Ghata was presumably not trying to evoke in her French original, but which are also less exact than they could have been: 'Seen' would have been a better option than 'Sin'. In this respect, Hacker's otherwise excellent translation is hampered by her lack of familiarity with Arabic, the ever-present shadow language in Khoury-Ghata's poems.

The poems of 'The Seven Honeysuckle Sprigs of Wisdom' focus on the inhabitants of a Lebanese village, with characterisations of the villagers which are frequently humorous as well as surreal: 'In my village the sheep are so tall they graze on the bellies of clouds, chew in / the violets' shadows while slandering Mansour the wool-carder.' Lebanon's complex cultural identity is touched on as well as the theme of language. The fate of a plum tree is, mysteriously, 'linked to the country's independence' and the narrator asks if it will 'answer to a name that perhaps won't suit its branches used to/ conversing with the Arab wind'.

Khoury-Ghata's narratives are lively and inventive, engaging elliptically with her themes of life, death and language. Nearly everything, animate or otherwise, is endowed here with a linguistic faculty of a sort: 'The books we browsed in came from the forest that watched us read.' There are many voices in *Alphabets of Sand* and such narration resists univocal histories,

making it particularly suitable for writing about Lebanon, with
its complexities of religious and ethnic identity. Whilst retaining
a sense of origin, these poems capture a polyglot aesthetic which is
well adapted to the subject matter. The lyrical beauty of Khoury-
Ghata's surreal, sensuous images and her evocation of Lebanon
as a landscape of anarchic, contesting alphabets, leave the reader
enchanted by a unique narrative voice.

Rowyda Amin

**The Other Half of History: An Anthology of Francophone
African Women's Poetry**
Translated and edited by Georgina Collins
Heaventree Press,
138pp, paperback, £9.99
ISBN 978 1 906038 10 6

Bending the Bow: An Anthology of African Love Poetry
Edited by Frank M Chipasula
Southern Illinois University Press
352pp, paperback, $22.95
ISBN 0 8093 28482 0

In both these valuable anthologies, the editors confront the near-
impossibility of representing the poetry of an entire continent.
   They do so in quite different ways. Frank Chipasula limits his
thematic scope, but within that, attempts to be as compendious
as possible. Georgina Collins, by contrast, has collected poems
over a wide subject range, but only those written in French by
women. Her project is one of recovery and redress; while surveying
previous, Francophone, African anthologies, she notes that '. . .
many compilers have barely considered female writers as part of
their remit' (p.xxi).
   Her introductory essay is enlightening on the task of linguistic

and cultural translation and excitedly anticipates future discoveries, as her on-going project builds '. . . a colourful, intricate and ever-changing collage . . .' (p. xxv). To counter the felt dearth of material from some regions in Africa, she includes biographical notes on the twenty-nine authors, a select bibliography of their works, a 'Further Reading' list, and helpful notes that set many of the poems' cultural context for the reader.

The poems themselves display an invigorating aesthetic and thematic variety. Werewere-Liking Gnipo gives History itself a voice ('A knot upside down / A knot on the edge / . . . / I am History'), Reine de Medeiros exhorts the Nation of Benin to be productive ('Long Live Production!'), while Marie Léontine Tsibinda engages with the legacy of colonisation and slavery ('The Road to the Stars'). Anna Gréki describes her beloved 'Algiers the White' in a beautiful cascade of similes, while Rosalie Aadama Tall harnesses the tradition of praise poetry ('Praise for My Oxen'). Joyce Mansour, member of the Surrealist movement, is represented – and contemporary writers continue the testing of form and meaning. Dorra Chammam's 'The Dance of the Passers-by' begins in forthright anger, but becomes something much stranger; dream-like and threatening:

Oh! To be, to be, to be...
To be cherry
Blackcurrant, blackberry, cyanide . . .
To be a red beret . . .
To suck from the beaks of sitting ducks
To be a dove . . .

Assia Djebar explores the entanglement of personal and linguistic identity in the rhythmic, tightly-structured 'Bound Hands':

My poetry is only murmurs
The robin's call or the sound of copper

Flee from the hole in my Arab veil
Even when I weave a French tale
I hear my foreign tongue again

The Other Half of History is a bilingual edition, allowing the
reader to follow the translator's choices. No such opportunity
is afforded in *Bending the Bow*; perhaps a minor casualty of the
editor's need to balance his anthology's ambition against its
portability.

Chipasula has opted for an historical perspective, with Ancient
Egyptian preceding the Traditional Love Songs, followed by
Modern and Contemporary Love Poetry (the largest section).
His anthology is impressively wide-ranging, taking in not only
languages such as Tamazight, Swahili, Arabic but also French,
Portuguese, English and including writers resident in the continent
as well as those from the African Diaspora. The introductory
essay is a helpful survey of the terrain – both geographically and
historically – and the book contains ample bibliographic and
biographical details of the authors, from which a reader could
embark on a fuller study of their work.

Bending the Bow contains many beautiful treasures. I was struck
by the vivid immediacy of the Ancient Egyptian love songs,
anonymously authored and often narrated by a woman. 'My Love
is Back, Let Me Shout Out the News' revolves around its central
image, where 'heart pirouettes in its dark chamber / glad as a fish
when night shades the pool'.

It's worth noting that Love Poetry here means heterosexual,
romantic, sexual love – but within that proscription, there is a
multiplicity of ways in which to address and describe the Beloved.
Dan Wylie in 'Loving This Younger Woman', addresses her as
'My whetstone, my bright / onyx!' Then she is 'like the moon
she is so/ mannered, angelic in her taught/ orbit, her magnesium
glow'. What would otherwise be a familiar comparison between
the lover and the moon is made strange by that 'magnesium' and
the emphasis placed on 'orbit' by the line break. Patricia Jabbeh
Wesley likens the lover to a quick succession of emphatically

African images; a 'Kissi ritual mask', 'pungent, leafy voodoo', to name but two. Léopold Sédar Senghor, founder of the Négritude Movement, employs a succession of verdant and striking natural images in 'I Will Pronounce Your Name': 'mild like cinnamon . . . the sugared clarity of blooming coffee trees . . .'. 'I Have Spun a Song Soft' is more tentative in its address to the lover, ending 'I have offered you my wild flowers. Will you let them wither, / Finding distraction in the mayflies dancing?'

Frustratingly, the poems' translations are patchily credited. It's left to the reader to discover from the Credits and Contributors' Notes that Siriman Cissko, for example, writes in French. The translator of his exuberant 'Tulip' ('I cry aloud the blue palm tree of your lashes . . .') remains unknown. A more stringent, final proof-reading might also have ironed out the occasional infelicity: the repetition of a phrase in the introduction; a lack of indents where some poems' longer lines spill over to the line beneath. Such inconsistencies are perhaps evidence of the enormity of the editor's task in compiling such a comprehensive collection.

The Other Half of History and Bending the Bow both seek to redress a balance, by bringing to light topics and voices previously neglected in African poetry. In doing so, they highlight the complexity of African poetic traditions and practices, proving themselves essential texts in the challenge to Eurocentricism. They are important additions to any poetry bookshelf.

Meryl Pugh

*An Anthology of Modern Italian Poetry, in English
Translation, with Italian Text*
Edited and translated by Ned Condini; introduction and notes
by Dana Renga
The Modern Language Association of America
464 pp $11.95
ISBN 978-1-60329-032-6

Annamaria Ferramosca
Other Signs, Other Circles: a Selection of Poems 1990-2009
Translated and introduced by Anamaria Crowe Serrano
Chelsea Editions $20.00
ISBN 978-0-9823849-2-3

In 1914, two years before his death, the poet Guido Gozzano
began publishing a series of 'entomological epistles', all of which
evoked various species of butterfly in a manner at once melodious
and exact. The collection, entitled *Le farfalle* (*Butterflies*), remained
unfinished at his death. Though not much read nowadays, these
late poems exhibit a passion for classification typical of much
modern Italian poetry. Italian poets cluster in movements, some
of which remain permanent chrysalids, while others unfurl
brief but vivid wings; there are 'Twilight poets' (*I crepuscolari*),
Futurists, Hermeticists, 'Fragmentists' (and 'Anti-Fragmentists'),
and 'Decadentists' – not, as it happens, a group of versifying
orthodontists but the coterie to which Gozzano himself belonged
– as well as, inevitably, 'Neo-Crepusculists'. Not even *Ornithoptera
pronomus* (one of Gozzano's favourite butterflies) was more firmly
pinned to its label than the typical twentieth-century Italian
poet.
    One of the strengths of Ned Condini's new anthology is to
demonstrate just how little these obsessive labels mean. The
thirty-eight poets included here display a truly impressive
unruliness. Presented chronologically, beginning with the
great Giovanni Pascoli (1855–1912), and concluding with poets
still active today, such as Edoardo Sanguineti and Giorgio

Guglielmino, the anthology attests to the robust vitality of Italian verse. Though Montale, Ungaretti, Saba and other major poets are well represented, lesser known poets, some of them translated for the first time into English, appear too; it is good to find Aldo Palazzeschi, Giorgio Caproni, and Mario Luzi, a great poet scarcely known outside Italy, in Condini's selection. And for once, women poets are well represented; not only Maria Luisa Spaziani, but Antonia Pozzi, Christina Campo and Amelia Rosselli, among others. Inevitably, there are imbalances: Cesare Pavese, Vittorio Sereni, and Leonardo Sinisgalli – three significant poets – have been excluded without explanation while Gian Pietro Lucini, a tedious blowhard, enjoys thirty or so pages and Pier Paolo Pasolini, an interesting poet, if not a great one, has forty.

Condini's translations are extremely uneven. He is most successful when most literal; though sometimes, as in his version of Gozzano's celebrated 'Totò Merúmeni' (in which 'fur-decked aliens rap on the Gorgon knocker'), he catches the staccato sonorities of the Italian. All too often, however, he falls into the well-known pitfalls of verse translation: padding, forced rhymes, and skewed syntax in particular. Thus, in straining to reproduce Pascoli's 'L'assiuolo' ('The Great Horned Owl'), he can write:

Puffs of lightning did shoot
from black clouds far below;
from the fields rose a call:
hoot, hoot.

And it gets worse, concluding with 'and still that dirge-like toot – *hoot, hoot* . . ."' – less a 'Great Horned Owl' than a candidate for *The Stuffed Owl*. Too many of his translations read almost like parodies of the originals. D'Annunzio isn't always as silly as Condini makes him sound: 'Some toss flowers about, some bandy mots,/ some muse on dainty thoughts' (or should that be 'thots?'). His versions of Montale are especially poor. He turns the wonderful early poem 'Meriggiare pallido e assorto' into a shrill jingle where 'cicadas raise quivering/ creaks from the barren peaks'. In another poem Montale writes of 'il bollore della vita fugace', literally, 'the boiling of fleeting life', which Condini turns into 'the stew/ of fleeting life'. It is the wrong register and distorts the tone of the original. Unfortunately, these are not isolated examples. It's a pity that so interesting a selection should be marred by so many false notes.

The remarkably original contemporary poet Annamaria Ferramosca is also missing from Condini's anthology. Happily, a representative selection of her work is now available, superbly translated by Anamaria Crowe Serrano. Ferramosca is a biologist by profession; she delights in technical terms but is mischievous enough to subvert these even as she glories in them. Her poems are simultaneously precise and intoxicated. Not all of her neologisms succeed; even her translator has a hard time with 'messapicagrecaegizialibica' (which becomes 'greekmessapicegyptianlybian'). But this matters little. Her poems, for all their bristling nomenclature, display a passionate urgency which carries even her wildest flights; one senses a living presence beneath the verbal extravagance, that of a woman 'with rebellious hair' and 'a vixen's muzzle'. Her scientifically trained eye gives her an unexpected compassion for the smallest things, as in 'Sometimes You See':

> As if set
>   in the rotting door
> a trembling moth (part of its wing cut off,
> a tiny missing piece of the mosaic)
> awaits its end,
>   soaks up one last ray
> Deaf to the invitations
> it knows to obey the ritual
> With dignified unsteadiness
> the veil already across its eyes
>   blurring memories
> already the lights of the afterlife
>   are dazzling
> (from afar they're celebrating the saint's feast day)

The same 'dignified unsteadiness' characterizes Ferramosca's best poems; they move with rather startling ease from small foibles, such as her own recurrent absentmindedness, to larger, more sinister concerns:

> Increasingly I forget
> where I've parked the car
> the streets look all the same
> with their sense of the sea encroaching
> with the confusing call of stones
> from the last riverbed

Ferramosca, perhaps unsurprisingly for a biologist, has something of a microscopic eye, alert to 'tiny infinite angstrom/ bioholds' but she uses these privileged glimpses of the infinitesimal as a way of evoking vaster presences, deep space as well as the deep time of myth and prehistory; in her work, the least droplet summons up the sea. I suspect that her penchant for joining words together, often violently, in dense compounds, comes from this same passionate fascination for extremes. But Ferramosca also commands a strong singing line – skilfully captured in Serrano's translations – and it is this which gives her finest poems their unmistakable accents:

> We are almonds of light in the cup of darkness
> little stubborn vibrations
> we'll leave traces of our mooring
> a trembling embrace in a shelter

All too predictably, Ferramosca has been linked with 'Neo-Orphism'. It seems safe to say that this is one butterfly that won't be pinned quietly to a board.

Eric Ormsby

Yang Lian
Lee Valley Poems
Translated by Brian Holton & Agnes Hung-Chong Chan, Jacob
Edmund, Polly Clark, Antony Dunn, W.N. Herbert, Pascale
Petit, Fiona Sampson, Arthur Sze with Yang Lian.
Bloodaxe Books,
111 pp, paperback, bilingual text, £9.95,
ISBN: 987-1-85224-834-5

Yang Lian was born in 1955 in Switzerland where his father was
in the diplomatic service, grew up in China and then when he
heard he was going to be arrested escaped to Europe in 1993
and has been living in London since 1997. He is now a poet of
international significance with many publications. This book is
one of his latest works.

In one of the *Lee Valley Poems* Yang Lian has the line 'the Tang
dynasty like a lantern suddenly switched on' where he looks back
to the great period of Chinese poetry with what I take as a fierce
pride, a sense of loss and a determination to make it new. Several
of the Chinese poets of the great dynasties found themselves out
of favour at court and were sent to exile in provincial towns or
perhaps to border postings where Chinese speakers were few.
Yang Lian escaped from China to a West which has limited
knowledge of Chinese and of the great poetry of China, a deeper
exile to bear.

In his excellent preface 'A wild goose speaks to me' he explains
how London has become gradually familiar to him and is the first
'local' he has had since he left China; how in London 'external
places are converted into my inner self to become part of the 'I' of
the text; and how ' "local" doesn't at all signify a specific site, but
must point to all sites, as being the ability of the poet to excavate
his own self'. He has also said 'exile is not so much a subject
matter as a depth, inside the poet's demand on language'.

His response is a poetry of fragmentation and darkness.
Fragments, but what fragments!

Whether the golden fish sing about the rise and fall of the
   city or not
a line of swans on the riverbank study the book of their
   feathers

('Stroller')

At the circle's centre, a text secretly watches me
draft another page.
My bed circles – floating in a ghost script
revealed then unravelled by water.

('The Journey')

one line of Chinese poetry lets the rain empty a room even
   more

('What Water Confirms')

He wants to establish a creative link between his own work
and the great works of the past. He admires the great poets Du
Fu who drifted from place to place and Qu Yuan who posed his
Question to Heaven and then took his own life.

The translations of the poems into English are with three
exceptions the result of close collaboration between the poet and
the translator, and my impression is that the results get as close
as can be expected to what the poet wrote in the Chinese. One
of the translators, Brian Holton, has written about the extreme
difficulty of translating Yang Lian's work, finding it almost
impossible to translate directly into English without losing all
the allusions in the Chinese characters which also depend on tone
and pitch. Yang Lian has explained how the languages of the
West are time-bound by the tenses in verbs and other indicators
of time whereas Chinese characters have no time association
and so are better able to carry the infinite. It is essential to the
poet to capture this timelessness in his writing so that much of
the poetry uses the present tense in the English translation. To
me the fragmentation in the English translations implies some
of the allusiveness of the original Chinese characters as well as

the Chinese text. In Yang Lian's essay *In search of Poetry as the 'Prototype'* he writes 'European languages seek to explore the concrete, Chinese is abstract.'

The images the poet uses are very precisely chosen and he remembers where each one came from. These images and observations drawn from the marshes do not accumulate in the way that Jorie Graham, for example, accumulates her details. Rather Yang Lian's details in all their simplicity and complexity flash into a room or wait outside as though they are parts of us. There is much more dark than light in his work. He writes 'exile has given me an inescapable perspective, which I daily deepen by writing . . . The effort to explore the ultimate limits of darkness can never be exhausted.' As I write this review in late November I feel the need for more light in the short days. I wish that same light for him.

Roger Moulson

Further Reviews

Al-Sayegh, Adnan
The Deleted Part, translated by Stephen Watts and Marga
    Burgui-Artajo
Exiled Writers Ink
32 pp, paperback, ISBN 978-0-9530971-5-9

Mukhopadhyay, Sarat Kumar,
The Cat Under the Stairs, translated by Robert McNamara
The Eastern Washington University Press
152 pp, paperback, ISBN-13: 978-1-59766-039-6, $15.95

Sen, Sudeep
Arias, Translations
Mulfran Press
150 pp, hardback, ISBN 978-81-88330-26-7

Godrej, Dinyar, editor
Fire in the Soul
New Internationalist Publications,
142 pp, paperback, ISBN 978-1-906523-16-9, £9.99

Nikolov, Lyubomir,
Unreal Estate, translated by Miroslav Nikolov
Carnegie Mellon Univ. Press,
pp72, paperback, ISBN 978-0-88748-497-1

Hamilton, Lucy,
Sonnets for My Mother
Hearing Eye,
40 pp, paperback, ISBN 978-1-905082-51-3 £4.00

With the Chilcot Inquiry's first round of public hearings on
Britain's involvement in Iraq coming to an end this month, it
seems fitting to begin this edition's round up with the refreshing

transparency of the Iraqi poet Adnan Al-Sayegh. *The Deleted Part* charts the poet's trajectory of exile and includes poems written across decades and cities including Beirut and Stockholm: 'Iraq disappears with/ every step its exiles take'. Born in Al-Kulfa in 1955, Al-Sayegh's distinct voice came to prominence in the 1980s. With already ten collections of poetry existing in Arabic, this modest chapbook was produced as part of Exiled Writers' Mentoring and Translation Programme. It offers an enigmatic introduction to poems often seen as 'slightly contentious' such as the delicate 'Night Prayers' which resulted in threats by armed militia to cut off the poet's tongue after a Poetry Festival in Basra in 1996:

> you see
> your god only
> in blades and blood
> I perceive Him
> in a word &
> a song & in
> the blue of her
> eyes & the sea ('Night Prayers')

Translated with a sense of humility by Stephen Watts and Marga Burgui-Artajo, the language is taut and tender as though written on the very skin of poetry. Al-Sayegh often confronts the complacency in which truth and poetic freedom are all too often taken for granted.

Sarat Kumar Mukhopadhyay's well-documented insistence on honesty being the poet's job explains the uncompromising edgy quality to the poems in his latest collection, *The Cat Under the Stairs*. Mukhopadhyay's cool gaze hovers over his subject matter and is unfettered by notions of ethnicity, and yet responds respectfully and philosophically to the everyday lives of those that surround him.

Whose side do you choose?
The rich, taking more than their due,
Tossing scraps to the poor, and tossing you too? ('To God')

Mukhopadhyay's mix of reportage and colloquial tone is a feature of many of the poems. Often he is at his best when the language borders on being enigmatic, wry and stark as in the sequence of poems titled 'Stress Series' confirming that these poems are not landlocked but freely transgress traditional and Western-influenced Bengali poetic traditions.

Celebrating South Asia's new generation of poets and preserving the integrity of texts by established voices are both primary concerns behind Sudeep Sen's highly praised book of translations. *Aria* is a truly collaborative achievement that brings to light Sen's passion for community and commonality. Sen anchors the reader with a generous essay that reveals his early beginnings and his process as a cosmopolitan translator. His starting point is a tri-lingual dance between Bengali, Hindi and English which he extends to a musical intimacy with the further languages that he encounters by translating alongside his peers. The effect produces over 100 poems that are sincerely and methodically realized.

Whether translating Rabindranath Tagore or Zoran Anchevski, Sen remains faithful to a theory of translation, which aims: 'to render accurately both the content and form of the original'. Sen questions the validity of 'transcreation', which to his mind may not have the 'efficacy' of the original poem. Sen's own attempt at transcreation with Mithu Sen's poem-sequence 'Bahia', creates a welcome shift of energy that perhaps signals future adventures in translation for Sen. A provocative guidebook for Sen may be Robert Lowell's 'free translations' anthology *Imitations* or Don Paterson's stance on versions of Antonio Machado in *The Eyes* (1999): 'It should surely, by now, be axiomatic that poetry cannot be translated in a way that will preserve anything of the flavour of the original.'

Sudeep Sen stands shoulder to shoulder with Peter Cole and

Dinah Livingstone whose translations feature in the recent
Amnesty and New Internationalist Anthology: *Fire in The Soul:
100 poems for Human Rights*. Dinyar Godrej's editorial choices
ensure an accessible journey through an array of injustices and
triumphs. This is largely due to the absence of poems with 'an
overbearing emphasis on craft; such poems can make reading
them a chore'. Godrej's editorial stance raises the issue of whether
working with 'difficulty' and 'formal constraints' are not in
themselves vital forms of protest.

Overall, the careful ordering of new and well-known voices
creates a powerful choral effect in a book that lends itself to
being experienced in one sitting. The effect is humbling, and
breathtaking highlights include John Felstiner's translation of
Paul Celan's 'Death Fugue' with the slow infusion of German
within the English repetitions, and the highly patterned poem
'Rich Woman, Poor Woman', written by an unknown working-
class Chilean woman.

The inclusion of biographical notes for each contributor sheds
light on the literary context, and enables the reader to appreciate
the struggles of the individual lives behind, and contained within,
the poems. Collectively these poems engage unflinchingly with
the complexity of human nature, the shadow side, and the light.

The tentative exploration of living in exile and the necessity
of living within one's heart is at the core of Lyubomir Nikolov's
most recent book *Unreal Estates*. No stranger to *MPT*, six of
Nikolov's poems were featured in the 'Diaspora' issue (3/2, 2004),
and seamlessly reside within a rich and unassuming collection.
Currently residing in the United States, Nikolov's homeland
Bulgaria becomes a blueprint from which the poems draw their
structure and form. The lyrical lilt of the line endings sing back
to folk song tradition and yet there is also a larger sense of the
poems living in eternity. Some of the shorter poems are best read
in the early light of day, the images wake the senses into being:

They follow the sun
stumbling in green clods of dirt,
they get up and walk,

holding their lanterns high.   ('Sunflowers')

Elsewhere, darkness is a welcome relief, and a place for
contemplation:

In the dark, existence has no aim.
Nests of mud – distant stars fall.
And everything to which you have sworn
betrays you with passion, love and pleasure.
                                        ('In the Dark')

A melancholic tone resounds quite poignantly within poems,
and yet the view is never bleak but expansive and hopeful, as
in the image of a half-asleep son in the final verse of the poem
'Fatherhood':

His right knee
touches my chest.
I need some light.
I get up and raise the blinds
a few inches, enough to write:
'Just like that the stars in the sky
cling to one another and don't plummet.'

Not only is a moment of closeness explored with such clarity of
thought and purpose, Lyubomir Nikolov also lives with the acute
awareness of the potential loss of those tender moments, his own
remedy is to allow words, images and language to confirm his
existence:

A dragonfly darts over water.

The blackberry – a drop of dark honey

And I, neck drawn out about the grass
am once again a poet.   ('Summer')

The closing stages of familial relationships are neverending. Even
within the slightness of the pamphlet form, the complexities
of putting feeling into words in Lucy Hamilton's *Sonnets for My
Mother* resonate beyond the crafted thirty sonnets. Spanning
a five-year period, the sonnets sequence acts, in this case, as a
reassuring structure to chart the decline of the narrator's mother
from a debilitating illness. Hamilton largely succeeds in her
ambition to integrate fragments of French songs and nursery
rhymes, alongside a playful subtle rhyme scheme. There are
thoughtful allusions and communion with texts such as Eliot's
Collected Poems and Elizabeth Smart's poetic prose novel *By Grand
Central Station I Sat Down and Wept*. Hamilton undoubtedly
writes with a grief-stricken eye and ear, and what she observes in
her own international language students is revealed as her own
journey:

    . . . She's trying to reach
    the shades of meaning in this written picture

    of seasons, ripening fruits and changing trees,
    all her mother's colour, music and culture
    vibrate through everything she thinks and sees.'
                        ('With All Her Mother's Colours')

A defining moment is reached in the honest delivery of the
penultimate sonnet. Here the poem lets go of the ambition of the
form and leaves the emotional map work of the sequence behind
and opens quietly with the lines: 'It was the little tongue that
struck me most/ in mum's last hours, tiny like a little bird's'. The

true strength of Hamilton's work lies in the tangles of desire for the mother tongue, denied in childhood and still withholding in the last stanza:

> I longed to touch her tongue. It seemed to be
> the key to understanding the interplay
> of vivid life and dark eternity.   ('In Her Presence')

Within the cocoon of impending grief, Hamilton skilfully wrestles with the suddenness of bereavement, which coincides with memories of 9/11 and the anniversary of a departed sister. 'Annette's Birthday' is a carefully enacted sonnet where public and private mourning momentarily meet. This begs the question, What is more realistic and achievable: that solace can be found in the rooms and corridors of the sonnet sequence, or that truth can be upheld in the rooms and corridors of power?

(See *MPT* 3/8 for Lucy Hamilton's sonnet version of *Lalla Maghnia*.)

Saradha Soobrayen

Notes on Contributors

Timothy Allen, born in Liverpool in 1960, has spent much of his life as a development worker in various parts of Africa, Latin America and Asia. In 2008, his translation of the opening lines of *Kiêu* was awarded a Stephen Spender Prize for Poetry in Translation; in 2009, a Hawthornden Fellowship enabled him to complete the translation of the whole text. He currently teaches EAP at the University of Liverpool.

Rowyda Amin won the Wasafiri New Writing Prize in 2009. Her pamphlet will be published by tall-lighthouse in 2010.

Paul Batchelor was born in Northumberland. He recently won the 2009 Edwin Morgan International Poetry Prize and the 2009 Times Stephen Spender Prize for Translation. His first collection, *The Sinking Road*, appeared in 2008 from Bloodaxe. See www.paulbatchelor.co.uk

Josephine Balmer is a poet and classical translator. Her latest collection, based on Ovid's *Tristia*, is *The Word for Sorrow* (Salt 2009).

Martin Bennett works as a teacher, translator and part-time proof-reader at the University of Tor Vergata in Rome. Some of his translations, mostly from the Italian, have appeared in previous issues of *MPT*, in *Stand*, *Poetry London* and other magazines.

Alison Brackenbury's seventh collection is *Singing in the Dark*, Carcanet, 2008. She has recently produced a chapbook of new animal poems, *Shadow*, available from www.happenstancepress.com. New poems can be read at her website: www.alisonbrackenbury.co.uk

Stephen Capus studied Russian Language and Literature at Birmingham University and undertook research on the Russian poet Marina Tsvetaeva at the School of Slavonic and East European Studies in London. He has published poems, translations and reviews in various periodicals, including *Slavonic and East European Review*, *Acumen* and *Agenda*.

Alex Cigale's poems have appeared in *The Colorado, Green Mountains, North American,* and *St. Petersburg* reviews, *Drunken Boat, McSweeney's, Redactions,* and *Zoland Poetry.* His translations can be found in *Crossing Centuries: the New Generation in Russian Poetry* and in *The Manhattan, St. Ann's, Yellow Medicine* reviews, and Brooklyn Rail In Translation. He was born in Chernovtsy, Ukraine and lives in New York City.

Murray Citron spoke Yiddish as a child in New York and Toronto, but largely lost the language when he went to school. Recently he came on the poetry of Itzik Manger, and is recovering the language to read the poems.

Dániel Dányi is a twenty-nine year old Hungarian translator and poet from Budapest. His translations include András Mezei's poems in *Holocaust Remember!,* Tom Wolfe's *The Electric Kool-Aid Acid Test,* and poems by D.H. Lawrence. He has published English-language poetry in *Pilvax* magazine.

Alan Dent is a poet, translator and critic. He edits the radical cultural journal *Penniless Press.* His anthology of contemporary French counter-cultural poetry, *When the Metro is Free,* is published by Smokestack.

Maureen Duffy is the author of thirty-one published works of poetry, fiction and biography as well as other works of non-fiction, and plays for stage, screen and radio. She is a fellow of the Royal Society of Literature and of King's College London.

William I. Elliott has lived some forty of his seventy-eight years in Yokohama, teaching literature at Kanto Gakuin University. His books include criticism and thirty translations of Japanese poetry, ancient and modern. With colleague Kawamura Kazuo he has translated fifty-four collections of Japan's best-known living poet, Tanikawa Shuntaro. Elliott has published seven collections of his own poems, most recently *An Evening's Entertainment* (2009).

Ruth Fainlight has written libretti for the Royal Opera House and Channel 4 TV, as well as many books of poems and two volumes of short stories. Her *Collected Poems* will be published by Bloodaxe Books next Autumn, and her translation of Sophocles' *Theban Plays* (in collaboration with Robert Littman) was published in the USA by Johns Hopkins University Press last spring.

Marilyn Hacker is the author of twelve books of poems. Her ten volumes of translations from the French include Marie Etienne's *King of a Hundred Horsemen* (Farrar Strauss and Giroux 2008), Vénus Khoury-Ghata's *Alphabets of Sand* (Carcanet Press 2009) and Emmanuel Moses' *He and I* (Oberlin College Press 2009). She is a Chancellor of the Academy of American Poets.

Paul Harris learnt Latin and Greek at Westminster School under the inspirational tuition of Theo Zinn. He subsequently changed to Chinese studies. He then pursued a career of over thirty years as a translator in the financial sector. Now, with the freedom that comes with retirement, he regularly spends a certain period of the year as a volunteer English teacher in China.

William Heath was born in London in 1980 and is a graduate of Bretton Hall College. He is self-taught in the Ancient Greek language and over the last few years has been working on the fragments of Archilochos, Alkman, Sappho, Alkaios, Ibykos, Hipponax, Stesichorus and Anakreon.

Norbert Hirschhorn is an international public health physician commended by President Bill Clinton as an 'American Health Hero'. He lives in London and Beirut. His poems have been published in many journals, anthologies, pamphlets, and two full collections. See his website, www.bertzpoet.com.

W.D. Jackson (b. Liverpool, 1947) has lived and worked in Italy and, since 1973, in Munich. The first two books of his work-in-progress, *Then and Now – Words in the Dark* (2002) and *From Now to Then* (2005) are published by Menard Press. *Boccaccio in Florence* came out recently from Shearsman / Menard.

Ilmar Lehtpere is the translator of six books of poetry and prose by Kristiina Ehin, most recently *The Scent of Your Shadow*, which will be published by Arc in 2010. He has begun work on a new trilingual Estonian-English-Scottish Gaelic volume of Kristiina Ehin's poetry. His own poetry has appeared in Estonian and Irish literary journals.

Arthur McHugh comes from Glasgow and now lives in Birmingham. He has published poems and translations in periodicals throughout the UK.

Rowan Middleton's work has appeared in *The London Magazine*, *Obsessed with Pipework* and the anthology *Desire and Madness*. He won the 2008 Francis Close award for creative writing and is currently studying at the University of Gloucestershire.

Hubert Moore's seventh full collection, *Happiness crouching there*, is to be published by Enitharmon in 2011.

Roger Moulson's first book *Waiting for the Night-Rowers* published by Enitharmon won the Aldeburgh Prize and was nominated for the Guardian First Book Award. His second collection is forthcoming.

Zuzanna Olszewska is a Junior Research Fellow in Oriental Studies at St. John's College, Oxford University. She recently completed a doctorate in Social Anthropology on *Poetry and its Social Contexts among Afghan Refugees in Iran*. She is working on further translations of Afghan poetry and an Afghan novel.

Eric Ormsby has published six collections of poetry, including *Facsimiles Of Time*, a volume of essays on poetry and translation. Carcanet will publish a new selection of his poetry in 2011.

Thomas Ország-Land is a poet and a foreign correspondent based in Eastern Europe. He is also a Jewish survivor of the Holocaust and the 1944-45 siege of Budapest. He participated in the 1956 Hungarian Uprising as a young journalist on the staff of *A Magyar Függetlenség*. His many books include *Tales of Matriarchy*, *Berlin Proposal*, *Prince Bluebeard's Castle* (a translation of the libretto of Bartók's opera) and *Deathmarch: Holocaust Poetry Translated from the Hungarian of Miklós Radnóti*.

Nasrin Parvaz's activities in human and civil rights in Tehran led to her imprisonment in Evin Prison from 1982 to 1990. Her book about her prison experience, *Beneath the Narcissus*, has been published in Farsi and Italian.

Pascale Petit's fifth collection *What the Water Gave Me – Poems after Frida Kahlo* (Seren, 2010) is published in May 2010. Her latest is *The Treekeeper's Tale* (Seren, 2008). Two of her books were shortlisted for the TS Eliot Prize and have been featured in Books of the Year in the *Times Literary Supplement* and the *Independent*. She teaches creative writing at Tate Modern. Website: http://www.pascalepetit.co.uk and Blog: http://pascalepetit.blogspot.com

Meryl Pugh participated in the 2009 Aldeburgh Poetry Festival Masterclass. Her pamphlet *Relinquish* was published in 2007 by Arrowhead Press; her poems have appeared recently in *New Welsh Review*, *Poetry Review* and *The Rialto*.

Shazea Quraishi was born in Pakistan, grew up in Canada and lived in Madrid before moving to London where she works as a writer, teacher and translator. Her poems have been published in anthologies and magazines in the UK and the US. She is working on her first collection.

Oliver Reynolds was born in Cardiff in 1957. He is an usher at the Royal Opera House. His four books of poetry include *Almost* (Faber 1999).

Maurice Riordan's most recent collection, *The Holy Land* (Faber 2007), received the Michael Hartnett Award. Previous collections, *A Word from the Loki* and *Floods*, were nominated for the T.S. Eliot Prize and the Whitbread Award. Other books include *Hart Crane*, which appeared in Faber's 'Poet to Poet' series. Born in Lisgoold, Co Cork, he lives in London and teaches at Sheffield Hallam University.

Cecilia Rossi holds an MA in Creative Writing from Cardiff University and a PhD in Literary Translation from the University of East Anglia. She has taught Literary Translation at MA level at both Middlesex University and the University of East Anglia. Her translation of Pizarnik's *Selected Poetry* is forthcoming from Waterloo Press.

Carol Rumens is the author of fifteen collections of poems, among them *Poems, 1968–2004* (Bloodaxe Books) and *Blind Spots* (Seren 2008). Her translations of Pushkin, Yevgeny Rein, Ratushinskaya and others appear in various anthologies, and her own poems have been translated into Polish, Romanian and Russian. She is a part-time Professor of Creative Writing at the University of Bangor and Visiting Professor of Creative Writing at the University of Hull.

Carole Satyamurti has published five collections of poetry. Her sixth collection will appear from Bloodaxe in 2011. She received a Cholmondeley Award in 2000.

Cameron Hawke Smith was born in Cambridge and has degrees in Ancient Greek and Archaeology. He has worked as a teacher, extramural lecturer and museum curator, and is now a free-lance writer. Poems and reviews by him have been published by West Midlands Arts, *PN Review*, *Acumen*, and Suffolk Poetry Society.

Saradha Soobrayen is the Poetry Editor of *Chroma*, a LGBT Literary Arts Journal. Her poetry appears in the *Red Anthology* 2009, the *Forward Anthology 2008*, and *Oxford Poets Anthology 2007*. She received an Eric Gregory Award in 2004.

Siriol Troup read French and German at St Hugh's College, Oxford and later returned there to teach 19th and 20th century French Literature. Her second collection, *Beneath the Rime*, was published by Shearsman in 2009.

Cristina Viti's recent translations include poetry by Elsa Morante (*MPT* 3/7; *Shearsman Magazine* 2009) and Stephen Watts (*L'Immaginazione*, Manni Editori 2008; Hearing Eye 2008), as well as texts by Tahar Lamri and Ubax Ali Farah (forthcoming in *Scarf,* Kudu Arts 2010).

Jonathan Waley has a degree in Chinese from the University of Cambridge. *His Spring in the Ruined City* (*Selected Poems of Du Fu*) was published by Shearsman in 2008. His website—www.jonathanwaley.co.uk contains further information about the book and his wider Chinese interests.

Gregory Warren Wilson's fourth collection, *The Mercury Fountain* (Enitharmon 2008) received an Arts Council award. He has tutored at The National Gallery, Tate Britain, and for the Arvon Foundation. He performs internationally as a classical violinist, and divides his time between London and Venice.

Robert Wilton is a writer and Balkan specialist. He was advisor to two Prime Ministers of Kosovo in the years leading to her independence; he is co-founder of The Ideas Partnership, which stimulates and supports projects in education, cultural heritage and the environment. His Balkan analysis and his short fiction have been widely published; he has just completed the first of a new series of historical espionage thrillers.

MPT Subscription Form

Name	Address
Phone	Postcode
E-mail	Country

I would like to subscribe to *Modern Poetry in Translation* (please tick relevant box):

Subscription Rates (including postage by surface mail)

	UK	Overseas
❑ One year subscription (2 issues)	£19.90	£25 / US$ 38
❑ Two year subscription (4 issues) with discount	£36	£46 / US$ 69

Student Discount*

	UK	Overseas
❑ One year subscription (2 issues)	£16	£21 / US$ 32
❑ Two year subscription (4 issues)	£28	£38 / US$ 57

Please indicate which year you expect to complete your studies 20 . . .

Standing Order Discount (only available to UK subscribers)

❑ Annual subscription (2 issues)	£18
❑ Student rate for annual subscription (2 issues)*	£14

Payment Method (please tick appropriate box)

❑ **Cheque:** please make cheques payable to: *Modern Poetry in Translation*. Sterling, US Dollar and Euro cheques accepted.

❑ **Standing Order:** please complete the standing order request below, indicating the date you would like your first payment to be taken. This should be at least one month after you return this form. We will set this up directly with your bank. Subsequent annual payments will be taken on the same date each year. For UK only.

Bank Name	Account Name
Branch Address	❑ Please notify my bank
	Please take my first payment on
Post Code	......./......./......... and future payments on
Sort Code	the same date each year.
Account Number	Signature:
	Date........./........./............

Bank Use Only: In favour of Modern Poetry in Translation, Lloyds TSB, 1 High St, Carfax, Oxford, OX1 4AA, UK a/c 03115155 Sort-code 30-96-35

Please return this form to: The Administrator, Modern Poetry in Translation, The Queen's College, Oxford, OX1 4AW administrator@mptmagazine/www.mptmagazine.com